**NORTHEAST
DOCUMENT
CONSERVATION
CENTER**

HANDBOOK FOR DIGITAL PROJECTS:

A Management Tool for Preservation and Access

First Edition

Maxine K. Sitts, Editor

**Northeast Document Conservation Center
Andover, Massachusetts, 2000**

The Institute of Museum and Library Services, a federal agency that fosters innovation, leadership, and a lifetime of learning, supported the publication of this book, ***Handbook for Digital Projects: A Management Tool for Preservation and Access,*** by the Northeast Document Conservation Center.

The National Endowment for the Humanities, an independent grant-making agency of the federal government, provides substantial funding to support field service activities, including publications, at the Northeast Document Conservation Center.

Library of Congress Cataloging Number
ISBN No. 0-9634685-4-5

Handbook for Digital Projects:
A Management Tool for Preservation and Access

Table of Contents

IX. DIGITAL LONGEVITY

Howard Besser, University of California, Los Angeles
School of Education & Information Studies

X. SCHOLAR COMMENTARY: AN END-USER SPEAKS UP

Charles Rhyne, Reed College

Preface

NEDCC is pleased to present this handbook to the professional community. Realizing there was very little literature on this pressing topic, the Northeast Document Conservation Center undertook the job of developing a guide to managing digital conversion projects. The goal was to produce an easy-to-use primer focused on meeting the information needs of libraries, museums, archives, and other collection-holding institutions. This manual is intended to serve as a resource and response. The main challenge was to compile and deliver the most up-to-date and useful information as soon as was possible. The project had to proceed on a tight timetable in order to bring to our readers information that was timely, and with recognition that it would not long remain so.

The publication builds on NEDCC's highly successful series of School for Scanning conferences, which it has offered on a national basis since 1996 with support from The Mellon Foundation and NEH. The publication includes chapters by a number of the conference faculty members and parallels the conference themes. Like the conference, the publication combines a tutorial on technical issues with an overview of larger issues, including the need for preservation of digital products. It begins from the premise that investing in digital conversion only makes sense if institutions are prepared to provide long-term access to digital collections.

NEDCC hopes this manual will help institutions to plan projects that build in considerations of quality and access over time. I would like to thank Maxine Sitts, who served as the incredibly efficient editor of the handbook; Steve Dalton, NEDCC's Field Service Director, who served as project manager; and Kim O'Leary who served as Webmaster. I would especially like to thank the Institute of Museum and Library Services, who supported the production of the handbook through a National Leadership Grant. I am also grateful for the National Endowment for the Humanities' support of NEDCC's Field Service Office.

Ann Russell
Executive Director, NEDCC

I
Introduction

This handbook is the product of four years of developing and revising curricula for School for Scanning conferences presented throughout the U.S. by the Northeast Document Conservation Center (NEDCC). The handbook provides a cumulation of tips, guidance, and advice from institutions that have engaged in digital projects. Taken in its entirety, it brings together information on best practices and summarizes lessons learned from many experiences. The approach, while managerial, is also practical and based on actual projects.

School for Scanning Conferences

School for Scanning conferences, funded by The Andrew W. Mellon Foundation and the National Endowment for the Humanities, were geared for administrators within cultural institutions, as well as librarians, archivists, curators, and other cultural or natural resource managers responsible for paper-based collections (including photographs). Keeping pace with developments, the conferences prepared participants to make critical decisions regarding the management of digital projects.

The conferences proved highly successful. Each attracted full-capacity audiences, with an average attendance of 300 persons per event. One factor leading to the popularity of the school was the continuity of the faculty — all practicing preservation-and-access professionals. These faculty members, in consultation with NEDCC staff, have prepared this handbook, drawing upon their conference presentations between 1996 and 2000. The ongoing dialogues at the School for Scanning provided the authors with unique opportunities to update and distill the ever-changing information about digitization based on the expressed needs of institutions whose primary goal is to protect, preserve, and provide access to the materials that document our cultural and historical heritage.

Purposes

Because only a few hundred individuals could attend each School for Scanning, which created waiting lists for the events, the Institute of Museum and Library Services agreed to support NEDCC's production of this handbook to reach broader audiences.

The handbook serves as a management tool for institutions concerned with preservation-and-access issues. It can help administrators and staff make informed decisions about:
- Determining the appropriate time and circumstances for digitization
- Integrating preservation needs into scanning projects
- Selecting materials for scanning
- Working with outside vendors
- Maintaining quality control
- Developing indexing and navigation tools and building databases
- Providing network access.

NEDCC expects that the handbook will prove useful for a variety of institutions — archives, museums, historical societies, and libraries of all types — and that it will speak to all levels of staff. This print version will prove particularly useful for individual learning at the introductory to intermediate level, for group planning sessions, and for reference as digital projects are planned and executed. The handbook is also available on the Web, where information will be regularly updated.

The goals established for the development of the printed and Web-version were to:
- Gather information on best practices for digitization of retrospective collections as they emerge from the practice of several large research libraries, and disseminate this information to small and medium-sized institutions
- Develop a teaching tool to support future training
- Maintain a Web version that will serve an even broader audience and be easily searchable
- Balance access concerns with concerns of preservation.

An Overview of the Contents

The handbook begins with an overview of the rationale for digitization and preservation that provides a foundation for understanding the preservation implications of digital conversion projects. The next chapter provides managers a clear understanding of the decisions that are typically under their control so they can form effective strategies to design, fund, and manage digitization projects.

The chapter on selection presents a three-stage process for selecting and prioritizing appropriate materials for digital work. It emphasizes the importance of good selection techniques to ensure that resources are invested wisely. The chapter on copyright offers a brief overview and introduction to the range of issues to be considered in any scanning or online project. Next, a technical primer focuses on the technical concepts and terminology that project management must know in order to make informed decisions, whether a project is conducted in-house or with vendors. Then, a series of case studies focuses on the practical results from scanning projects that dealt with: printed text and manuscripts, photographs, optical character recognition (OCR), maps and other oversize documents, microfilm, and cooperative endeavors. The Vendor Relations chapter discusses how vendors can be located, evaluated, and monitored, and offers guidance on developing Requests for Information and Requests for Proposals. The next chapter looks into the future — the issues of long-term preservation and the problems of digital longevity. Of particular interest, it explores how our community can contribute to efforts to preserve digital information. A final chapter gives the perspective of a scholar-researcher and end-user of digital materials.

Some authors have included checklists or questionnaires to be used as tools for planning and overseeing projects, as well as lists of resources.

This Handbook . . .

- Interprets digital technology from the perspective of the unique needs of institutions charged with safeguarding and providing access to cultural treasures

- Explores how institutions can justify digital imaging projects

- Describes how to manage projects so as to support the institution's basic goals and mission

- Stresses the need to consider preservation when digitizing — and explains how to do so

- Advises on how to deal effectively with vendors

- Emphasizes the importance of evaluating projects

- Encourages institutions to share their experiences.

Tips

- Remain true to the mission and goals of the institution in digital projects

- Take as much time as is needed at the outset of a project to clearly define its goals and outcomes

- Insist on the highest quality technical work that the institution can afford

- Build-in costs and capabilities for long-term maintenance of the digitized materials

- Cultivate a high level of staff involvement for digital projects

- Cooperate with other institutions whenever possible to achieve the greatest benefits

- Share experiences and results with other institutions.

Authors

Howard Besser, Associate Professor, University of California, Los Angeles, School of Education & Information Studies

Stephen Chapman, Preservation Librarian for Digital Projects, Harvard University Library

Paul Conway, Head, Preservation Department, Yale University Library

Eileen Gifford Fenton, JSTOR Production Manager, University of Michigan

Franziska Frey, Imaging Scientist, Image Permanence Institute

Janet Gertz, Director for Preservation, Columbia University Libraries

Melissa Smith Levine, Esq., Library of Congress National Digital Library Project

Steven Puglia, Special Media Preservation Branch, National Archives and Records Administration

Charles Rhyne, Professor and Art Historian, Reed College

Steve Smith, Editor, *Microform and Imaging Review* and former Imaging Service Coordinator, Amigos Library Services Inc.

Diane Vogt-O'Connor, Senior Archivist, Museum Management Program, National Park Service

Editor: Maxine Sitts, Communications Consultant, San Leandro, CA

Contributor (Chapter VI): Don Willis, President, eGroup, LLC, and Connetex Consulting

II
Overview: Rationale for Digitization and Preservation

Paul Conway
Yale University Library

This chapter provides a foundation for understanding the preservation implications of digital conversion projects. Following a brief description of the advantages and disadvantages of digital technologies, the author defines preservation in the digital context and describes how the underlying principles of traditional preservation practice relate to the creation of digital products. The key to successful digital conversion programs is the relationships among three concepts: (1) the purposes that the digital products will serve, (2) source document characteristics, and (3) technology capabilities brought to bear during the conversion process. At the heart of the digital conversion enterprise is this author's assertion that "preservation is the creation of digital products worth maintaining over time." Preservation in the digital context is separate from but integrally related to preservation actions taken on original source materials. The chapter ends with a reiteration of the idea of *responsible custody,* a highly relevant idea articulated over fifty years ago to describe the central role of preservation in cultural institutions.

Introduction

In *Motel of the Mysteries,* illustrator David Macaulay (1979) speculates about how people 2,000 years from now might interpret the cultural significance of a low-budget roadside motel, **Toot 'n C'mon,** buried intact under junk mail and pollution. Beyond being a wry satire on the science of archeology, the book is a clever reminder of the danger of trying to interpret the past without documentary evidence. A *Do Not Disturb* sign becomes a sacred seal "placed upon the handle of the great outer door by the necropolis officials following the closing of the tomb." A charge card becomes "a portable shrine which was to be carried through life and into eternal life." A television represents "the essence of religious communication." Archeologists and historians know that the impulses to record and to keep are practically a part of our human nature. Truth is embedded in the symbols and artifacts that we create and then keep by choice or by accident. And yet, as the 21st century dawns, we find ourselves potentially confronting the dilemma of Howard Carson, Macaulay's amateur digger: a vast void of knowledge filled by myth and speculation. Information in digital form, the newest currency of our world, is more fragile than the fragments of papyrus found buried with the Pharaohs.

Digital imaging is 'hot.' Major daily newspapers devote entire sections on emerging trends in digital technology. Notwithstanding the results of recent surveys of the Web showing that the overall proportion (83%) of Internet content is commercial in character and that only six percent is educational or informational, the perception persists that everything of value is becoming digital or created in that form.

Digital images are indeed becoming commonplace in libraries and archives. The quality of digital image products can be spectacular. There is little doubt that quality will improve as the technology matures. Organizations are rearranging budgets, raising money, and anticipating income streams to make digital projects happen. Can any institution — library, archives, historical society, or museum — afford to squander this investment? Without serious effort to ensure long-term access to today's digital image files, however, the risk of loss is tremendous.

Preservation is not just for the world of paper. We know that digital imaging technology, in and of itself, provides no easy answers to the preservation question. Indeed, simply defining what preservation means in the digital imaging environment is a challenge. Responding to the insight that such a definition might provide is harder still. The digital world poses significant challenges to, but does not eliminate the need for, responsible, effective preservation activity (Waters & Garrett, 1996).

Advantages of Digital Access

Digital imaging technology offers distinctive advantages to institutions with impressive collections of scholarly resources. Information content can be delivered directly to the reader without human intervention. Information content in digital form can be retrieved by readers remotely, although such delivery may tax the capabilities of even the most sophisticated projection equipment and networks. Digital image quality is extraordinary and is improving constantly. It is now possible to represent almost any type of traditional research material with such visual quality that reference to the original materials is unnecessary for most, if not all, purposes. The power of full-text searching and sophisticated, cross-collection indexing affords readers the opportunity to make new uses of traditional research resources. Newly developed system interfaces (the look and feel of the computer screen) combined with new ways to deliver manageable portions of large image data files promise to revolutionize the ways in which research materials are used for teaching and learning. It is no wonder that there is a nearly overwhelming rush to jump on the digital bandwagon.

Risks of Digital Imaging Projects

Pressures from all fronts to digitize traditional research materials carry distinctive risks. The required investment for digital image conversion is tremendous — possibly dollars for each and every page or frame converted. Digital imaging technologies require tremendous capital investment for underlying support systems in an environment of flat or marginally increasing budgets. Digital image conversion, in an operational environment, requires a deep and longstanding institutional commitment to traditional preservation, the full integration of the technology into information management procedures and processes, and significant leadership in developing appropriate definitions and standards for digital preservation.

The risk of loss is high — far higher than in most other programs and activities carried out in a cultural institution. The nearly constant swirl of product development that fuels our perceptions of change raises the stakes higher still. When a library, archives, historical society, museum, or any other cultural organization with a preservation mandate stops experimenting with digital technology and decides to use it to improve services or transform operations, that institution has embarked down the preservation path.

What Digital Imaging Is Not

In the past few years, significant progress has been made to define the terms and outline a research agenda for preserving digital information that was either "born digital" or transformed to digital from traditional sources. "Digital preservation refers to the various methods of keeping digital materials alive into the future," according to a recent statement from the Council on Library and Information Resources (Waters, 1998). Digital preservation typically centers on the choice of interim storage media, the life expectancy of a digital imaging system, and the expectation to migrate the digital files to future systems while maintaining both the full functionality and the integrity of the original digital system. PBS recently aired the film *Into the Future,* which graphically portrayed the problem of digital information and speculated widely on the consequences of inaction, all the while offering precious few ideas of what to do about the dilemma.

It may be premature for most of us to worry about preserving digital objects until we have figured out how to make digital products that are worth preserving. Digital imaging technologies create an entirely new form of information from traditional documents. Digital imaging technology is not simply another reformatting option in the preservation tool kit. Digital imaging involves transforming the very concept of format, not simply creating a faithful reproduction of a book, document, photograph, or map on a different medium. The power of digital enhancement, the possibilities for structured indexes, and the mathematics of compression and communication together fundamentally alter the concept of preservation in the digital world. These transformations, along with the new possibilities they place on information professionals, force us to transform library and archival services and programs in turn.

Preservation in the Digital World

The essence of traditional preservation management is resource allocation. People, money, and materials must be acquired, organized, and put to work to prevent deterioration or renew the usability of selected groups of materials. Preservation largely is concerned with the evidence embedded in a nearly endless variety of forms and formats. Things are preserved so that they can be used for all kinds of purposes, scholarly and otherwise.

People with the responsibility to do so have determined that some small portion of the vast sea of information, structured as collections of documents, books, collections, and other things, has research value as evidence well beyond the time and way intended by those who created or published it (Buckland, 1991). This distinction between the value of the information content (usually text and illustration) and the value of the evidence embedded in the artifact is at the heart of a decision-making process that is itself central to the effective management of both traditional and digital library materials.

In the digital world, preservation is the creation of digital products worth maintaining over time.

Each of these words carries weight.
- IS. Preservation is a reality and not merely a metaphor for or symbol of access.
- CREATION. The time to be concerned about the long-term persistence of digital products is when a system is designed and before digital conversion has begun.
- PRODUCTS. A digital product has its own identity and exists within a market economy. It is not necessary to sell or license a digital product for the product to have an identity within a community of end-users.
- WORTH. The work to design and create a digital product adds value to the information contained in the documents that serve as sources. The value added to a digital product must ultimately result in a product that is an essential and vital capital resource to the institution that has chosen to create it in the first place.
- MAINTAINING. The persistence of digital products requires careful attention to the maintenance of content (the bits and bytes) functionality (how the bits work in a system).
- OVER TIME. Preservation in the digital world is not absolute, but depends instead on the continuing transformative impact of the digital product on the information work of end-users.

It is impossible to come to terms with the responsibilities inherent in creating digital products without distinguishing between acquiring digital imaging technologies to solve a particular problem and adopting them as an information management strategy. Acquiring an imaging system to enhance access to library and archives materials is as simple as choosing the combination of off-the-shelf scanners, computers, and monitors that meets immediate functional specifications. Hundreds of cultural organizations already have invested in or are planning to purchase digital image conversion systems and experiment with their capabilities. Innumerable pilot projects have shown how much more challenging it is to digitize scholarly resources than the modern office correspondence and case files that drove the technology two decades ago. In time, most of these small-scale, pilot projects will fade away quietly — and the initial investment will be lost — as the costs of maintaining these systems become apparent, as vendors go out of business, and as patrons become more accustomed to remote-access image databases and the latest bells and whistles.

Administrators who have responsibility for selecting systems for converting materials with long-term value also bear responsibility for preserving their investment in the product. This commitment is a continuing one — decisions about preservation cannot be deferred in the hope that technological solutions will emerge like a medieval knight in shining armor. An appraisal of the present value of a book, a manuscript collection, or a series of photographs in its original format is the necessary point of departure for making a judgment about preservation of the digital image version. The mere potential of increased access to a digitized collection does not add value to an underutilized collection. Similarly, the powerful capabilities of a relational index cannot compensate for a collection of documents whose structure, relationships, and intellectual content are poorly understood. Random access is not a magic potion for effective collection management.

Relationships Among Purpose, Source, and Technology

The key to a successful conversion project or ongoing program lies in a thorough understanding of the relationships among three concepts. These concepts are (1) the characteristics of the source material being converted, (2) the capabilities of the technology used to accomplish the digital conversion, and (3) the purposes or uses to which the digital end product will be put. The figure that follows illustrates these relationships.

The Preservation Purposes of the Digital Product

It is possible to distinguish among three distinctive but not mutually exclusive preservation applications of digital technologies, defined in part by the possible purposes that the products may serve for end-users.

Protect Originals. The most common application of digital technologies in an archive or library is digital copies that can be used for ready reference in lieu of casual browsing through the original sources. Preservation goals are met because physical access to the original documents is limited. Examples include image reference files of photograph, clipping, or vertical files that permit the identification of individual items requiring closer study. The original order of the collection, or a book, may be frozen much like microfilm sets images in a linear array. This preservation use of the technology has become a compelling force motivating archives and libraries to experiment with hardware and software capabilities.

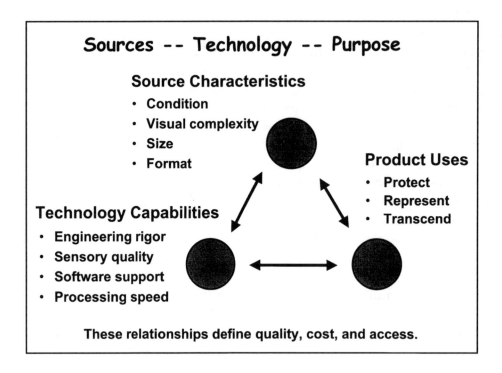

Represent Originals. A digital system could be built that represents the information content of the original sources in such detail that the system can be used to fulfill most, if not all, of the research and learning potential of the original documents. High-resolution systems that strive for comprehensive and complete content and seek to obtain full information capture, based on emerging standards and best practices, fit this definition. Systems of this intermediate level of quality open new avenues of research and use and could have a transformative effect on the service missions of those who create the products.

Transcend Originals. In a very small but increasing number of applications, digital imaging holds the promise of generating a product that can be used for purposes that are impossible to achieve with the original sources. This category includes imaging that uses special lighting to draw out details obscured by age, use, and environmental damage; imaging that makes use of specialized photographic intermediates; or imaging of such high resolution that the study of artifactual characteristics is possible. This category also includes digital imaging products that incorporate searchable full text (marked up or *raw*). Additionally, digital products that draw together, organize, and enhance access to widely dispersed research materials may have transcendental impact on the people who use them.

Each of these preservation applications places separate but increasingly rigorous demands on digital technologies. In each case, the use of an intermediate film or paper copy to facilitate the scanning process may or may not be necessary or advisable. Finally, the disposition of original sources (including undertaking preservation treatments before or after conversion) is a matter quite separate from the decision to undertake digital conversion. Ultimately, the purpose of digital image products is determined by the uses to which they will be put, while preservation of original source documents must be determined by their specific preservation needs.

The Characteristics of Source Materials Being Converted

A major challenge in choosing paths from analog to digital is obtaining an in-depth understanding of the particular characteristics of the collections or the individual items being converted (Robinson, 1993). The most important characteristics are:

- Format of the source (including size of object, its structure, and its physical condition)
- Physical condition and its impact on the ability of the item to be handled during the conversion process
- Visual characteristics (including the centrality of text versus illustration)
- Color as an essential carrier of information content
- Level of detail (including the size and style of typefaces, the type of illustrative content, and the overall range of tonal values).

Beyond these specific characteristics, the degree of visual and physical similarity among the individual items in a given collection can have a significant impact on the cost, quality, and complexity of the conversion project.

The Capabilities of Scanning Technology

The third key to building a viable digital product is the measurement of the capabilities of the digital imaging hardware/software system in relation to the source documents and the purposes of the product. Digital conversion systems vary widely in capability and cost. Rigorous mechanical and electrical engineering plays a big role in the design and manufacture of specialized conversion tools. Many products are optimized for the conversion of a single type of document. All conversion tools have limitations in terms of the size of source documents they can handle with a given level of digital resolution. Although the adage, "You get what you pay for" typically applies in the acquisition of conversion hardware, there is no substitute for careful and thorough testing and benchmarking of conversion systems (Besser and Trant, 1995).

The expected uses of the product may drive the choice of technological applications, but the opposite is not necessarily true. It is important to recognize that standards and best practices that support digital product development should not be driven by the present limitations of digital image capture, display, and output. Matters such as the limited resolution of today's display screens and projection devices, the limited bandwidth of wide and local area networks, and the limitations of resolution and tone reproduction in printers should not determine the quality thresholds of image system design.

The relationships among source characteristics, technology capabilities, and the purposes of the end product bear upon the definitions of quality, cost, and access. In the area of quality, for example, an input source with particular characteristics, the limitations or costs of scanning technology at a given point, and the expected uses of the product interact to set the threshold requirements for image quality. Similarly, the expected purposes of the digital product and the characteristics of the source interact with imaging technology capabilities to determine the cost of creating the product with the intended purpose. The same is true for access, where the intellectual complexity of the source documents and the specification for the ways in which the image product will be used interact with the sophistication (or lack of it) of the hardware and software tools for building metadata files and other associated indexes.

Transformation of Preservation Principles

In the past two decades, a consensus has emerged within a community of practitioners about a set of fundamental principles that should govern the management of available resources in a mature preservation program. The principles of preservation in the digital world are the same as those of the analog world, and, in essence, define the priorities for extending the useful life of information resources. These concepts are longevity, choice, quality, integrity, and accessibility.

Preservation in the digital world is one of the central leadership issues of our day. It is the shared responsibility of many people in many institutions fulfilling many roles. An understanding of the impact of this role differentiation on digital preservation action is crucial. Role differentiation helps archivists and librarians — acting as digital product developers — know when to control their use of digital technologies, when they need to influence trends, and when they need to relinquish any expectation for either control or influence.

The Transformation of Longevity
The central concern in traditional preservation practice is the media upon which information is stored. The top priority is extending the life of paper, film, and magnetic tape by stabilizing their structures and limiting the ability of internal and external factors to cause deterioration. The focus on *external* factors has led to specifications for proper environmental controls, care and handling guidelines, and disaster recovery procedures. Progress on efforts to control or mitigate the *internal* factors of deterioration has resulted in alkaline paper standards, archival quality microfilm, mass deacidification, and more rugged magnetic media. And yet, now that archivists and librarians have defined the issues surrounding the life expectancy of storage media, the very concept of permanence that has driven the

search for "archival" media is fading as a meaningful intellectual construct for preservation (O'Toole, 1989).

Preservation in the digital context has little concern for the longevity of optical disks and newer, more fragile storage media. The viability of digital image files depends far more on the life expectancy of the access system — a chain only as strong as its weakest component. Today's optical media most likely will far outlast the capability of systems to retrieve and interpret the data stored on them. Since it can never be known for certain when a system cannot be maintained or supported by a vendor, product developers must anticipate that valuable image data, indexes, and software will be migrated in their professional lifetimes to future generations of the technology.

Digital project managers can exercise a large measure of control over the longevity of digital image data through the careful selection, handling, and storage of rugged, well-tested storage media. They can influence the life expectancy of the information by making sure that local budgetary commitments are made consistently at an appropriate level. Ultimately, they have no control over the evolution of the imaging marketplace, especially corporate research and development activities that have a tremendous impact on the life expectancy of the digital systems created today.

The Transformation of Choice

Choice is selection. Preservation adds value through the process of selection. Choice involves defining value, recognizing it in something, and then deciding to address its preservation needs in the way most appropriate to that value. Over decades the act of preservation has evolved from saving material from oblivion and assembling it in secure buildings to more sophisticated assessing of condition and value on already-collected materials. Preservation selection has largely been driven by the need to stretch limited resources in as wise a fashion as possible, resulting in the dictum that "no item shall be preserved twice." The net result is a growing virtual special collection of items preserved with a variety of techniques, most notably by reformatting on microfilm. Selection is perhaps the most difficult of undertakings precisely because it is static and conceived by practitioners as either completely divorced from present use or completely driven by demand.

Selection in the digital world is not a choice made once and for all near the end of an item's life cycle, but rather is an ongoing process intimately connected to the active use of the digital files (Hazen, 1998). The value judgments applied when making a decision to convert documents from paper or film to digital images are valid only within the context of the original system. It is a rare collection of digital files, indeed, that can justify the cost of a comprehensive migration strategy without factoring in the larger intellectual context of related digital files stored elsewhere and their combined uses for teaching and learning.

Even while recognizing that selection decisions cannot be made autonomously or in a vacuum, librarians and archivists can choose which books, articles, photographs, film, and other materials are converted from paper or film into digital image form. Influence over the continuing value of digital image files is largely vested in the right to decide when it is time to migrate image data to a future storage and access system and when a digital file has outlived its usefulness to the institution charged with preserving it. What digital product developers cannot control is the impact of their ongoing value judgments on the abilities of readers to find and use information in digital form. Unused digital products might as well not exist; they certainly will not survive for long as mere artifacts of the conversion process.

The Transformation of Quality

> **D**igital product developers must reclaim image quality as the heart and soul of preservation.

Maximizing the quality of all work performed is such an important maxim in the preservation field that few people state this fundamental principle directly. Instead, the preservation literature dictates high quality outcomes by specifying standards for treatment options, reformatting processes, and preventive measures. The commitment to quality standards — do it once, do it right — permeates all preservation activity, including library binding standards, archival microfilm creation guidelines, conservation treatment procedures, the choice of supplies and materials, and a low tolerance for error. The evolution of preservation microfilming as a central strategy for the bulk of brittle library materials has placed the quality of the medium and the quality of the visual image on an equal plane. In the pursuit of quality microfilm, compromise on visual truth and archival stability is dictated largely by the characteristics of the item chosen for preservation.

Quality in the digital world, on the other hand, is conditioned significantly by the limitations of capture and display technology. Digital conversion places less emphasis on obtaining a faithful reproduction of the original in favor of finding the best representation of the original with a given technology. Mechanisms and techniques for judging the quality of digital reproductions are different and more sophisticated than those for assessing microfilm or photocopy reproductions (Kenney & Chapman, 1996). Additionally, the primary goal of preservation quality is to capture as much intellectual and visual content as is technically possible and then present that content to end-users in ways most appropriate to their needs.

The image market has subsumed the principle of maximum quality to the "solution" that finds the minimum level of quality acceptable to today's system users. Digital product developers must reclaim image quality as the heart and soul of preservation. This means maximizing the amount of data captured in the digital scanning process, documenting image enhancement techniques, and specifying file compression routines that do not result in the loss of data during telecommunication. The control of digital quality standards is possible now, just as it is for microfilm. However, librarians and archivists can only influence the development of standards for data compression, communication, display, and output. Improvements in the technical capabilities of image conversion hardware and software are in the hands of the imaging industry.

The Transformation of Integrity

The concept of integrity has two dimensions in the traditional preservation context — physical and intellectual — both of which concern the nature of the evidence contained in the document. Physical integrity largely concerns the item as artifact. It plays out most directly in the conservation studio, where skilled bench staff use water-soluble glues, age-old hand-binding techniques, and high quality materials to protect historical evidence of use, past conservation treatments, and intended or unintended changes to the structure of the item. The preservation of intellectual integrity is based upon concern for evidence of a different sort. The authenticity, or truthfulness, of the information content of an item, maintained through documentation of both provenance — the chain of ownership — and treatment, where appropriate, is at the heart of intellectual integrity. Beyond the history of an item is concern for protecting and documenting the relationships among items in a collection. In traditional preservation practice, the concepts of quality and integrity reinforce each other.

In the digital world, maintaining the physical integrity of a digital image file has far less to do with the media than with the loss of information when a file is created originally, then compressed mathematically, stored in various formats, and sent across a network. In the domain of intellectual integrity, structural indexes and data descriptions traditionally published with an item as tables of contents or prepared as discrete finding aids or bibliographic records must be inextricably linked and preserved along with the digital image files themselves. Preserving intellectual integrity also involves authentication procedures, like audit trails, that make sure files are not altered intentionally or accidentally (Duranti, 1995). Ultimately, the digital world fundamentally transforms traditional preservation principles from guaranteeing the physical integrity of the object to specifying the creation of the object whose intellectual integrity is its primary characteristic.

Librarians and archivists can exercise control over the integrity of digital image files by authenticating access procedures and documenting successive modifications to a given digital record. They can also create and maintain structural indexes and bibliographic linkages within well-developed and well-understood database standards. Digital product developers also have a role to play in influencing the development of metadata interchange standards including the tools and techniques that will allow structured, documented, and standardized information about data files and databases to be shared across platforms, systems, and international boundaries. It is vain to think, however, that librarians and archivists are anything but bystanders observing the rapid development of network protocols, bandwidth, or the data security techniques that are essential to the persistence of digital objects over time.

The Transformation of Access

In the fifty years that preservation has been emerging as a professional specialty in libraries and archives, the preservation and access responsibilities of an archive or library have often been in tension. "While preservation is a primary goal or responsibility, an equally compelling mandate — access and use — sets up a classic conflict that must be arbitrated by the custodians and caretakers of archival records," states a fundamental textbook in the field (Ritzenthaler, 1993). The intimate relationship between preservation and access has changed in ways that mirror the technological environment of cultural institutions.

Preservation OR Access. In the early years of modern archival agencies — prior to World War II — preservation simply meant collecting. The sheer act of pulling a collection of manuscripts from a barn, a basement, or a parking garage and placing it intact in a dry building with locks on the door fulfilled the fundamental preservation mandate of the institution. In this regard preservation and access are mutually exclusive activities. Use exposes a collection to risk of theft, damage, or misuse of either content or object. The safest way to ensure that a book lasts for a long time is to lock it up or make a copy for use.

Preservation AND Access. Modern preservation management strategies posit that preservation and access are mutually reinforcing ideas. Preservation action is taken on an item so that it may be used. In this view, creating a preservation copy on microfilm of a deteriorated book without making it possible to find the film is a waste of money. In the world of preservation AND access, however, it is theoretically possible to fulfill a preservation need without solving access problems. Conversely, access to scholarly materials can be guaranteed for a very long period, indeed, without taking any concrete preservation action on them.

Preservation IS Access. Librarians and archivists concerned about the preservation of electronic records sometimes view the two concepts as cause and effect. The act of preserving makes access possible. Equating preservation with access, however, implies that preservation is defined by availability, when indeed this construct may be getting it backwards. Preservation is no more access than access is preservation. Simply refocusing the preservation issue on access oversimplifies the preservation issues by suggesting that access is the engine of preservation without addressing the nature of the thing being preserved.

Preservation OF Access. In the digital world, preservation is the action and access is the thing — the act of preserving access. A more accurate construct simply states "preserve accessibility." When transformed in this way, a whole new series of complexities arises. Preserve access to what? The answer suggested in this chapter is: a high quality, high value, well-protected, and fully integrated digital product that is derived from but independent of original source documents. The content, structure, and integrity of the digital product assume center stage — and the ability of a machine to transport and display this product becomes an assumed end result of the preservation action rather than its primary goal.

Control over accessibility, especially the capacity of the system to export digital image files (and associated indexes) to future generations of the technology, can be exercised in part through prudent purchases of only nonproprietary hardware and software components. In the present environment, true plug-and-play components are more widely available. The financial commitment by librarians and archivists is one of the only incentives that vendors have to adopt open system architectures or at least provide better documentation on the inner workings of their systems. Additionally, librarians and archivists can influence vendors and manufacturers to provide new equipment that is backward compatible with existing systems. This capability assists image file system migration in the same way that today's word processing software allows access to documents created with earlier versions. Much as they might wish otherwise, digital product developers have little or no control over the life expectancy of a given digital image system and the decision to abandon that system.

Conclusion

Fifty years ago, one of the foremost and persistent advocates for quality library bookbinding put his finger on the centrality of preservation to the mission of modern research libraries and archives. Preservation, wrote Pelham Barr in his most frequently cited work, "as responsible custody, is the only library function which should be continuously at work twenty-four hours a day. It is the only function which should be concerned with every piece of material in the library from the moment the selector becomes aware of its existence to the day it is discarded" (Barr, 1946).

Barr's allusion to the lifecycle of information sources is timeless. Today the concept is at the center of information management theory and practice, including specifications for the disposition of government archives, the management of book collections, and the maintenance of large-scale information technology systems. Responsible custody circumscribes preservation in the digital world as well, where the creation of digital products worth maintaining over time is the measure of success. The idea of responsible custody should govern actions as we build digital products vested with the value of intellectual endeavors.

Summary of Key Principles and Points

- Define clear boundaries for a digital conversion project, particularly the end point.
- Brainstorm: In nontechnical terms, state the desired outcomes for the source materials and the functional requirements for the digital reproductions.
- Justify why digital, rather than analog, reproduction is necessary.
  — Describe the audiences and their needs.
  — Describe the things that digital copies will do that analog copies cannot.
- Project a lifespan for the digital reproductions.

- Plan: Write a project plan, budget, timeline, and other planning documents.
- Budget and plan workflow based upon the results of scanning and cataloging a representative sample of material.
- Budget (time, if not dollars) for training.
- Implement: Coordinate simultaneous or overlapping workflows.
- Segregate materials into batches for conversion and quality control.
- Write documentation during the project.
- Report on the lessons learned, particularly the failures and blind alleys: help yourself and your colleagues to learn from your mistakes.

Sources

Barr, Pelham. "Book Conservation and University Library Administration," *College & Research Libraries* 7 (July 1946): 218-19.

Besser, Howard and Jennifer Trant. *Introduction to Imaging: Issues in Constructing an Image Database.* Santa Monica: Getty Art History Information Program, 1995. http://www.gii.getty.edu/intro_imaging/

Buckland, Michael K. "Information as Thing," *Journal of the American Society for Information Science* 42 (June 1991): 351-60.

Conway, Paul. *Preservation in the Digital World.* Washington, DC: Commission on Preservation and Access, March 1996. http://www.clir.org/cpa/reports/conway2/

Digital Imaging Technology for Preservation. Proceedings from an RLG Symposium Held March 17 and 18, 1994. Nancy E. Elkington, ed. Mountain View, CA: Research Libraries Group, 1994.

Duranti, Luciana. *The Preservation of the Integrity of Electronic Records.* School of Library, Archival, and Information Studies, University of British Columbia, 1994-97. http://www.slais.ubc.ca/users/duranti/intro.htm

——. "Reliability and Authenticity: The Concepts and Their Implications." *Archivaria* 39 (Spring 1995): 5-10.

Ester, Michael. *Digital Image Collections: Issues and Practice.* Washington, DC: Commission on Preservation and Access, 1996.

Frey, Franziska. "Digital Imaging for Photographic Collections: Foundations for Technical Standards." *RLG DigiNews* 1 (3), December 15, 1997. http://www.rlg.org/preserv/diginews/

Graham, Peter S. "Requirements for the Digital Research Library." *College & Research Libraries* 56 (July 1995): 331-39.

Hazen, Dan, Jeffrey Horrell, and Jan Merrill-Oldham. *Selecting Research Collections for Digitization*. Washington, DC: Council on Library and Information Resources, 1998. http://www.clir.org/pubs/reports/hazen/pub74.html

Kenney, Anne R. and Stephen Chapman. *Digital Imaging for Libraries and Archives*. Ithaca, NY: Dept. of Preservation and Conservation, Cornell University Library, 1996.

Levy, David M. "Heroic Measures: Reflections on the Possibility and Purpose of Digital Preservation." *Proceedings of the Third ACM Conference on Digital Libraries,*1998, pages 152-61. http://www.acm.org/pubs/citations/proceedings/dl/276675/p152-levy/

Lynch, Clifford. "The Integrity of Digital Information: Mechanics and Definitional Issues." *Journal of the American Society for Information Science* 45 (December 1994): 737-44.

Macaulay, David. *Motel of the Mysteries*. Boston: Houghton Mifflin, 1979.

Mohlhenrich, Janice. *Preservation of Electronic Formats: Electronic Formats for Preservation*. Fort Atkinson, WI: Highsmith, 1993.

O'Toole, James M. "On the Idea of Permanence." *American Archivist* 52 (Winter 1989): 10-25.

Reilly, James M. and Franziska A. Frey. *Recommendations for the Evaluation of Digital Images Produced from Photographic, Microphotographic, and Various Paper Formats*. Report to the Library of Congress National Digital Library Project. Rochester, NY: Image Permanence Institute, May 1996. http://memory.loc.gov/ammem/ipirpt.html

Ritzenthaler, Mary Lynn. *Preserving Archives and Manuscripts*. Chicago: Society of American Archivists, 1993, p.1.

Robinson, Peter. *The Digitization of Primary Textual Sources*. Office for Humanities Communication Publication, no. 4. Oxford: Oxford University Computing Services, 1993.

Rothenberg, Jeff. "Ensuring the Longevity of Digital Documents." *Scientific American* 272 (January 1995): 42-47.

Smith, Abby. *The Future of the Past: Preservation in American Research Libraries*. Washington, DC: Council on Library and Information Resources, 1999. http://www.clir.org/pubs/reports/pub82/pub82text.html

———. *Why Digitize?* Washington, DC: Council on Library and Information Resources, 1999. http://www.clir.org/pubs/reports/pub80-smith/pub80.html

Van Bogart, John W. *Magnetic Tape Storage and Handling: A Guide for Libraries and Archives.* Washington, DC: Commission on Preservation and Access, 1995.

Waters, Donald J. "Digital Preservation?" *CLIR Issues* (November/December 1998): 1. http://www.clir.org/pubs/issues/issues.html

———. "What Are Digital Libraries?" *CLIR Issues* 4 (July/August 1998). http://www.clir.org/pubs/issues/issues04.html

Waters, Donald and John Garrett. *Preserving Digital Information: Report of the Task Force on Archiving of Digital Information.* Washington, DC: Research Libraries Group and Commission on Preservation and Access, May 1996. http://www.rlg.org/ArchTF/

III
Considerations for Project Management

Stephen Chapman
Harvard University Library

Librarians and archivists are experts at project management. They routinely process groups of materials in selection, processing, cataloging, and preservation workflows. Digital projects, however, create new challenges. Perhaps the most difficult challenge is establishing clear boundaries, particularly stopping points. Managers of several noteworthy projects have written about their experiences in creating collections that require constant modification to keep pace with improvements in technology (Thomas, 1998).

This is not to say that digital conversion projects cannot be well planned in advance and successfully managed to conclusion. Many questions and challenges can be anticipated, and much of the workflow can be structured as batch activities with predictable outcomes. The purpose of this chapter is to give managers a clear understanding of the decisions that are typically under their control so they can form effective strategies to design, fund, and manage digitization projects.

Setting Goals

The best-managed conversion projects have clear goals. Brainstorming, the first phase of project management, is the time to talk about outcomes. "Starting at the end" is an effective way to ensure smooth beginnings. Too often there is a tendency to dive right into questions of technology — *e.g.,* which scanner should I buy? — before articulating the purposes that digital reformatting must serve. Setting goals is a process of thinking about things from several angles before writing project plans. What are the possible outcomes for the collections? What are the potential benefits to users, to collection managers, and to the institution? What is a reasonable price — in time and money — to invest in new procedures, systems, and services? Is self-publishing a good idea, or are partnerships (with other institutions or even publishers) a better course to follow? Is this the right time to begin digitizing collections?

Good management is largely an act of communication. If the people who work on the project understand the desired outcomes, they will provide better services; they will be aware of their individual contribution and how it relates to what others are doing; they will know why they are digitizing collections *(the vision thing);* and, perhaps most importantly, they will be better at recognizing when things go wrong.

The starting-at-the-end approach refers to focusing on outcomes before analyzing source materials or evaluating conversion processes. As described in the following sections, outcomes generally fall into three categories: collections, digital reproductions, and institutional benefits. Before writing a project plan and budget, bring together all of the stakeholders who have an interest in these issues and establish priorities that everyone can accept.

The Collections

When one speaks of preservation and access as project goals, there is a certain transitive quality to the statement. Digital conversion projects are undertaken on behalf of original collections. *(Original* is used here to refer to any source material for scanning, regardless of its format.)

A popular rationale for investing in digital collections is that the surrogates will reduce, if not eliminate, the physical handling that threatens fragile or unique materials (Noerr, 1999). This sounds sensible, but beware of the responsibility of advancing this logic. Remember that digital collections do not make themselves, and consider that a collection is likely to be handled more during conversion than at any other time during its life in an institution. Digitizing for preservation, then, applies not only to outcomes, but also to the handling guidelines that will be mandated for the conversion process. Remember, too, that increased care and handling generally translate to increased cost.

Once materials have been selected for conversion, one should articulate the specific physical outcomes desired for the source materials. Whenever the originals are to be removed from circulation — either by change in policy, transfer to offsite storage, or, more rarely, disposal — imaging requirements will be high. As noted in Chapter VII Section 1, "Working with Printed Text and Manuscripts," high quality does not necessarily refer to high cost, but quality control, authentication of files and their sources, and other issues become more critical in cases where original materials cannot be easily retrieved or consulted.

In all projects, whether digitization is to serve access goals, preservation goals, or both, consider the following questions:
- Will materials be assessed, treated, or conserved before being returned to storage?
- Will it be necessary, or desirable, to clean or stabilize materials prior to scanning?
- Is rehousing a goal?

- Will items be returned to their original locations or sent to off-site storage in order to recover needed space and/or to improve the storage conditions for the materials?

Other questions address access policies and cataloging.
- Following scanning, will formerly circulating items be assigned a noncirculating status?
- Will policies of access to archives and manuscripts be changed?
- Will surrogates be used for exhibits?
- If the goal is to improve access to the collections, then to what extent should the bibliographic description (*e.g.,* catalog records, finding aids) be enhanced?
- Do new records need to be created?
- Does the finding aid need to be encoded?

Stating the goals for the original collections first will make it easier to narrow the wide range of choices of scanning technologies and methodologies. With rapidly deteriorating source materials — such as newspapers, brittle books and journals, notebooks, and scrapbooks — a hybrid approach to conversion might be desirable. These undertakings demand planning for two, or even three, workflows, creating digital surrogates for access, creating microfilm for preservation, and, if necessary, rehousing or otherwise treating the originals.

The Digital Reproductions

There is not a one-size-fits-all approach to scanning because there are many types of source materials, diverse audiences with a wide range of interests, and an ever-expanding choice of digital formats. The most diligent student of technology — even as it relates to the field of digital libraries — will not be able to keep up with new or emerging products. Even when people are knowledgeable about digital formats, it is wise to prepare for a discussion about various strategies. Do not assume there will be ready consensus on what is best.

Ultimately the project manager, not the technology manufacturer or distributor, must be the one to judge whether a given system will do the job that is needed. Librarians and archivists, rather than engineers, have the skills to describe in practical terms what the digital reproductions are supposed to do. To paraphrase Michael Ester, President of Luna Imaging, Inc., formulating the rationale for digitizing a collection relies upon curators' abilities to exercise their own good judgment. Technology can then be assessed according to project objectives rather than *vice versa* (Ester, 1997).

There are two schools of thought about developing specifications for digital reformatting. One advocates closely assessing the source materials, then relating the attributes of the digital reproductions to those of the originals. This practice is sometimes referred to as benchmarking (Kenney, 1999). The other recommends that attributes of digital reproductions be related to those of the hardware and software systems that will display or process them. As an example, consider working with printed originals, such as papyri. Scanning to create a high-quality print may not necessarily satisfy the requirement to magnify details on screen at 10:1.

Characterizing functional requirements from the user's point of view can make the job of defining technical specifications much easier. What resources are available to the audience(s) you intend to serve? Answering this question is particularly vexing when you want digital collections to persist. What assumptions does one make about the systems people will have ten to twenty years from now? When thinking about all of the ways that technology can be used to enhance access to collections, consider:

- Who are the users or potential users of digital collections?
- How will they locate your collection, items within the collection, and relevant subsets of the item?
- If images are delivered to the screen, how will they be viewed? One at a time? Several together to facilitate comparisons? Will zooming be required?
- If printing is required, will images (or full-text) be delivered one page at a time or in appropriate-sized chunks?
- From your user's perspective, what constitutes legibility? Do colors need to be reproduced? If so, with accuracy to the original? Do the reproductions need to mimic contemporary (*e.g.,* faded) appearance, original condition, or both?

Benchmarking, by contrast, considers the interests of the collections' creators (original artists and publishers) and custodians to be as important as today's users. In this approach, the attributes of the source materials that need to be conveyed in the digital reproductions (either pictorially, in textual metadata, or both) are:

- Organization and presentation (collective value of a scrapbook page, for example; or side-by-side presentation of pages originally published in codex form)
- Size and dimension
- Detail, tone, and color
- Age and condition.

By adopting the user's and the owner's perspectives, the project manager will be in a better position to articulate project goals to staff and/or the vendors who offer systems and services. Successful working relationships can be established when representatives from cultural institutions can describe the functional requirements for the digital reproductions; representatives from industry can then respond with offerings of what technology can do — they may even be motivated to create new systems.

Perhaps the most important goal at this point of a planning exercise is to answer the following question: Can you state functional requirements that can only be fulfilled by digital reproductions? If not, reformat your collections with an appropriate analog process (National Endowment for the Humanities, 1999).

One final note about defining requirements for the digital reproductions: A lifespan, even if only approximated, should be assigned to the electronic editions to help define technical requirements for conversion as well as the overall project budget. With analog formats, we can take for granted that the institution will bear the ongoing costs to store, catalog, and provide access to the reproductions. The overhead for storage facilities and supporting technologies such as circulation systems, photocopiers, and microform readers is considered to be affordable.

With digital formats, interventions will be comparatively frequent, and maintenance can be defined anywhere on the scale of simple copying (to new media and/or new formats) to budgeting for wholesale digital-to-digital conversion in order to maintain a standard level of service. It is one thing to preserve content, another to preserve a level of service. All this is to say that longevity is not a physical attribute of digital reproductions, but an assigned lifespan that is backed up by the recognition that today's decisions regarding digital quality and functionality will need to be supported by tomorrow's managers and portions of their operational budgets.

Benefits to the Institution

In recent years, many organizations have invested in digital projects with an eye toward realizing institutional benefits, as well as enhancing access to their collections. Oxford University, for example, categorizes digitization projects according to four objectives: Access, Infrastructure, Preservation, and Feasibility (Lee, 1999).

Research libraries in particular have been interested in feasibility and infrastructure projects for several years. These are important parts of a collective effort to test and disseminate tools, procedures, and methodologies. Managers in organizations of all sizes are often interested in monitoring processes of first-time digitization projects in order to conduct cost-benefit analyses. The experience gained by doing projects in-house helps organizations understand the overhead not only in creating digital collections, but also in maintaining and delivering them.

The following quotes from those with real-world experience in managing digital projects illustrate how different institutional goals can lead to different philosophies about creating electronic collections (or *vice versa*):

> *As we evaluate new reformatting technologies, we can 'keep it simple' by working on large quantities of material with few problems before working on smaller quantities of material with difficult problems* (Waters, 1999).

> *If an electronic scholarly project can't fail and doesn't produce new ignorance, then it isn't worth a damn* (Unsworth, 1999).

In the former case, the KISS principle applies, and the logic is that solving small problems helps institutions prepare for tackling larger ones. In the latter case, the bigger problems are more appealing, as the certain failure will itself represent a meaningful stride towards developing expertise.

Experience can produce tangible benefits as well. These include:

- Distributing procedures and guidelines for use by the institution or contractors
- Integrating new digital management systems with existing catalogs and databases
- Instituting local services, such as electronic reserves, to enhance traditional ones
- Recovering space
- Establishing contractual relationships with publishing partners who will assist in creating and/or distributing digital content (see the *Costs* sidebar later in this chapter)
- Facilitating public relations and fundraising
- Raising revenue (if not full cost recovery) through sale of products (*e.g.,* from museums).

Project Planning: Creating a Plan of Work and Budget

Setting goals represents the thinking or brainstorming first phase of a project, and a good manager knows when to make the transition to planning, the second phase.

If a department or institution were to conduct only a single project — and provide all necessary funding — then it might be possible to skip planning and proceed directly to the work itself. The time invested in writing planning documents, however, will pay off during production. These documents are also fundamental stepping stones that lead from the first project to the second and third. If published, they also can serve as guideposts for other institutions planning digital conversion projects (Library of Congress, 1999). Examples of planning documents include:

- Request for funding (*i.e.,* grant application)
- A Request for Information (RFI)/Request for Proposal (RFP) if any conversion work will be contracted
- Job descriptions
- Procedures manuals (or instruction sheets) for selection, handling, scanning, metadata creation, and quality control
- Flowcharts or other workflow diagrams
- Data element lists
- A plan of work and project budget.

From the internal perspective, these early management documents may be the most important products to emerge from a project. Some of the documents, such as RFPs or contracts, will have a direct impact on product quality. The plan of work, by contrast, will have a direct impact on the processes to initiate, undertake, and complete the project.

Several elements are essential to the plan of work, regardless of the nature of the source materials or demands of the core audience(s) to be served. Specific answers to the five questions below help to ensure that fewer problems will be encountered when the work begins.

(1) Who will do the work?

Practically speaking, this question comes first because many of the tasks will have to be carried out by people already in the organization. When it comes to staffing, perhaps it is more accurate to survey the organization and ask, "Who is available to do this type of work?" or "Who has the right skills to learn to participate in a digital conversion project?"

The second phase of charting out the staffing picture is to determine how many new FTE will be required. Always assume that somebody will need to be hired to get the job done. No matter how small or simple the project appears, a good rule of thumb is "the job is always more than one person can do." Medium-scale projects require several departments to work together. Large projects require coordination among multiple agencies, institutions, service bureaus, and publishing partners.

Large projects not only have multiple positions but also several people with appropriate expertise in each job category. Small projects, by contrast, will not require a dozen full-time employees, but someone will have to assume these roles if the work is to be executed with reasonable levels of responsibility. (Naturally, several of these jobs can be subcontracted.) Each of the following roles, or tasks, is too important to be excluded from a project that seeks to convert materials, maintain them for any reasonable length of time, and make them accessible via computer networks (or even CD-ROMs).

Project Staff — Roles

- Project manager
- Selector
- Conservator, curator, or other analyst of the source materials
- Preparations technician (may also be curator, who, in turn, may also be the selector)
- Cataloger to create or enhance bibliographic records and to withdraw materials for conversion
- Scanning technician or photographer
- Quality control technician (may also be the scanning technician)
- Metadata analyst (may also be the cataloger)
- Data entry technician
- Programmer or other database expert who integrates metadata and images into a coherent resource (also known as the digital object)
- Systems administrator or other manager of electronic records and systems
- Network administrator to implement security and other access requirements (may also be the systems administrator)
- Developer or designer of the user interface

III. Considerations for Project Management

For each of the project staff roles, decide where training is needed, who will provide it, when it should (or must) occur, and how much it will cost.

(2) What systems will need to be used or developed during the project?
In this context, systems refer to software, hardware, and the good old-fashioned brick-and-mortar facilities needed to store media. Although highly flexible, digital products are physical objects that must be located somewhere. It is important to specify before work begins where the digital objects will be stored, how long they must reside there in readable and accessible form, and who will be responsible for them.

Software and hardware requirements will vary, but the number of systems will be proportionate to the number of processes and tasks specified to be under local control. In other words, the capabilities of the local infrastructure define the limits of the work that can be done in-house.

Consider the medium to long-term consequences that will result from the hardware and software decisions you are inclined to make on behalf of the short-term needs of the project. Will you be willing to build throw-away systems? Will it be acceptable to abandon custom applications when a programmer leaves? Or will commercial solutions be required?

(3) What are the technical specifications for the image files and metadata?
Digital images and associated metadata (in a number of categories) comprise the raw stuff of image databases. If consistencies in searching and presentation are desired, then it is essential to mandate technical specifications for data elements, image formats, and access protocols. These specifications become even more important when interoperability with other collections is desired.

Chapter VII describes some of the practices and specifications employed to date. If exact specifications cannot be determined before actually scanning or cataloging materials, then the project plan should at least state the options under consideration.

(4) How much will the project cost?
Empirical evidence gathered from one's own collections is more convincing than anecdotal reports from other projects. One of the best ways to forecast project costs is to create a representative sample of the materials selected for conversion. In many cases, a half dozen items will be sufficient. If scanning will be outsourced, then the project budget should be finalized only after a sample has been put through an entire workflow — scanning, processing, metadata creation (including full text), and quality control — and the results have been inspected and approved by the appropriate stakeholders in the project. Many vendors are willing to provide this service as part of their response to the RFI or RFP in order to compete for a contract.

All activities conducted in-house should be accounted for as project costs or cost share. An advance walk-through of the proposed workflows can quickly reveal how well the manager has envisioned the process from brainstorming map to reality. Surprises can occur. It may take a considerable amount of time to retrieve materials from storage and pack them for shipment to a vendor; this time must be doubled, of course, to account for the return phase. The digital masters that you intended to be inspected during a 100% quality control check may take five minutes to open on the computer you have available for this task. Catalog records that seemed adequate upon initial cursory review require clean-up or additional information. Try to identify in advance where production bottlenecks can occur and make sure that the levels of budget and staffing in the plan of work allow room for such contingencies.

Finally, consider the impact of a timeline on all of the project costs, particularly staffing when salaries and benefits must be budgeted for fixed periods.

(5) Who will own and manage the digital products that will be produced?
This question applies to staffing, workflow, and the budget. As noted in a *New York Times* article in April 1999, questions regarding storage "cannot be resolved without considering the question of ownership." In the same article, Ann Okerson of Yale University observed, "I don't know how you can preserve something you don't own" (Hafner, 1999). *Costs,* at the end of this chapter, shows the financial impact of taking on the responsibilities to store and deliver digital collections. Because of the high costs of infrastructure to manage and distribute digital objects, perhaps it is not surprising to see that a number of partnerships between university libraries and publishers have emerged. (*Early American Fiction* published by Chadwyck-Healey and the University of Virginia Library is a representative example.) If an institution desires to own and distribute the digital reproductions it creates for any length of time, then it will be important to articulate these goals in a project plan, to purchase the systems and staffing necessary to manage them, and to ensure that either the institution or the project's funder(s) will fully support these components as well.

Project Implementation: Managing Workflow

The third and final phase of project management is implementation. Virtually all digital conversion projects require several workflows to be charted and managed. One exception might be an in-house keying project with light encoding. Projects will be completed sooner if the tasks are orchestrated in parallel or overlapping rather than linear workflows. Cost may be the bottom line in the project budget and other planning documents, but time is what must be accounted for in managing the actual work of converting collections.

The following activities typically are segregated into separate workflows. Separate individuals or departments might end up undertaking each activity.
- Selection

- Copyright clearance or other research regarding rights and permissions; creation of rights and permissions metadata
- Preparation, including conservation assessment and/or treatment if necessary
- Creating catalog records, finding aids, or other pointers to a digital object or collection (descriptive metadata)
- Digital image production: Scanning source materials to create digital masters and associated technical medatata; processing master images to create derivatives for screen or print
- Check-in and quality control for source materials and digital images; transfer of sources to original or new location; rehousing materials, updating catalog records as necessary
- Creation of structural metadata
- Creation of full text, including mark-up
- File management: Loading data to repository
- Integration of digital images and metadata into an image database; hyperlinking associated catalog records or other access points
- Delivery: can range from hand-crafting web pages to relying upon a highly automated system
- Advertising, promotion, user evaluation.

Work would proceed more or less chronologically as listed above if materials were not segregated into batches during production. Selecting the appropriate size for each batch and following its progress carefully from start to end is the manager's principal responsibility. Gathering and reporting production statistics, problem logs, feedback from staff, and expenditures are all indicators of effective management.

When considering digital conversion from a hands-on perspective, it is easy to appreciate the efficiencies of working with batches of similar materials whenever possible. This is true for cataloging as well as scanning. If the materials themselves cannot be grouped in like categories, then work will often be structured in a series of steps, where technicians focus on specific tasks for meaningful, uninterrupted periods. With the appropriate configuration of a project facility, workers can be given the opportunity to break the repetitive cycle of one task (such as scanning) by moving to another (such as quality control and metadata creation). This practice facilitates high production and helps ensure consistent quality.

Guidelines and Best Practices for Management

One often hears about the need for best practices or guidelines for digital conversion. In the area of project management, the first measure of best practice is likely to be one of the ends justifying the means. If digital reproductions are well received and have been made in a timely and cost-effective fashion, the project will naturally be considered a success. Another measure, particularly from peer institutions and practitioners, might be in the quality of the documentation gathered throughout the project. Documenting the rationale, methodologies, systems, staffing models, costs, and most importantly, the lessons learned from a project helps the broader community (*i.e.,* within the institution, funders, and other practitioners) benefit from the experience gained in a single project. The project manager has done his or her job well if the people who worked on it had a satisfying experience and if the future manager(s) of the digital collection can easily interpret why things were created in a particular way and what needs to be done to maintain, or even to improve, these first-generation digital objects.

Costs

Costs are difficult to generalize due to the wide spectrum of digital processes and products. Even when source materials and digital reproductions are comparable, investments can vary considerably in activities such as project planning and management, as well as in the infrastructure to store and deliver digital objects.

Conversion Costs

Conversion is a bounded project activity, regularly outsourced to specialists. Production scanning, OCR, text markup, and digital photography costs are relatively predictable. Trends over the last several years suggest that text and image conversion costs will remain stable or increase slightly — not decrease — although product quality may be improving in several areas. The base numbers provided below should be construed as realistic starting points for budgeting. Increases over base are approximations of the impact of the combined variables introduced by the nature of the source materials as well as the technical specifications for the digital objects.

Product	Base Price	Meaningful Cost Factors	Increase (Over Base)
page images	$ .25/page	- size (page dimensions) - format (paper < microfilm) - binding (removed < intact) - bit depth (b/w < grayscale < color) - metadata (descriptive and structural)	2-6X (1-bit) 4-25X (8-24 bit)
full text	$ .50/page*	*same as for page images above, plus* - required level of accuracy - extent of markup ("lite" to full SGML)	6X + (keying) 2X + (markup)
images (pictorial)	$3.00/image	size (dimensions of originals) - handling requirements - tone/color reproduction requirements - metadata	2-20X

* includes cost of page images

Full Project Costs

Underscoring the point that conversion to digital is only one of the steps leading to delivery of digital, the Internet Library of Early Journals *Final Report* states that the cost "per indexed page image accessible on the Internet" is approximately seven times higher than the unit cost of scanning and uncorrected OCR (see Note below). Since libraries and archives are actively integrating digital technologies into acquisition, cataloging, systems, and even preservation departments, perhaps it is legitimate to consider these activities as costs that live outside of a conversion project. Nevertheless, it is important to recognize that analog-to-digital publishing (including distribution) requires significant investments — JSTOR and the Library of Congress National Digital Library Program provide two noteworthy, if large-scale, examples — to develop and integrate new systems, services, and expertise. Commercial publishers are willing to provide these services, but the terms of such agreements must be reviewed carefully to balance interests of project budgeting with those of collection ownership and control.

Note: "Internet Library of Early Journals (January 1996 - August 1998), A project in the eLib programme, *Final Report*." March, 1999. [http://www.bodley.ox.ac.uk/ilej/papers/fr1999/] (October 24, 1999). See, paragraph 80: "The total of £458,000 [approx. $757,395 USD] represents an expenditure of £4.21 [approx. $6.96 USD] per indexed page image accessible on the Internet. This estimate of expenditure does not take into account the costs of the contribution of the IT and library infrastructures of the four Institutions." See also page E14.

Sources

Borghuis, Marthyn, *et al. TULIIP Final Report*. Elsevier Science, 1996. See Appendix X, "Checklist of aspects to be considered for the implementation of a 'digital library,' 337-44.

Chapman, Stephen and Anne R. Kenney. "Digital Conversion of Research Library Materials: A Case for Full Informational Capture." See Table 4. *D-Lib Magazine* (October 1996). [http://www.dlib.org/dlib/october96/cornell/10chapman.html] (November 4,1999).

Ester, Michael. *Digital Image Collections: Issues and Practice*, pp. 10-12. Washington, DC: Commission on Preservation and Access, 1996.

Hafner, Katie. "Books to Bytes: The Electronic Archive, Research Libraries Grapple With the Difficult Task of Preserving the Digital Present." *The New York Times* on the Web. April 8, 1999. [http://www.nytimes.com/library/tech/ 99/04/circuits/articles/08arch.html] (November 4, 1999).

Internet Library of Early Journals (January 1996-August 1998), A project in the eLib programme, *Final Report*. March 1999. [http://www.bodley.ox.ac.uk/ilej/papers/fr1999/] (October 24, 1999).

Kenney, Anne R. "Digital to Microfilm Conversion: A Demonstration Project, 1994-1996, Final Report to the National Endowment for the Humanities, PS-20781-94." Also see other publications about the methodology used by the Cornell University Department of Preservation and Conservation. [http://www.library.cornell.edu/preservation/pub.htm] (October 24, 1999).

Lee, Stuart D. *Scoping the Future of the University of Oxford's Digital Library Collections, funded by the Andrew W. Mellon Foundation, Final Report*. Appendix D, 1. Oxford University, August 1999.

The Library of Congress, for example, has published many useful "Background Papers and Technical Information," available on-line, during the course of creating American Memory collections. See the Technical Operations Documentation and White Papers, n.d. [http://memory.loc.gov/ammem/ftpfiles.html] (October 24, 1999).

The National Endowment for the Humanities Division of Preservation and Access, for example, accepts applications for digital conversion projects, but holds these applications to the standard that. ". . . digitization [must] significantly improve access to the collection and the ways in which [it] may be used for scholarship, education, or public programming." See "Considerations for Reviewers," August 1999.

Noerr, Peter. *The Digital Library Tool Kit.* Sun Microsystems, Inc. (April 1998): 21.
[http://www.sun.com/products-n-solutions/edu/libraries/ digitaltoolkit.html]
(October 24,1999).

Puglia, Steven. "The Costs of Digital Imaging Projects." *RLG DigiNews.* 3:5 (October 15, 1999).
[http://www.rlg.org/preserv/diginews/diginews3-5.html#feature] (November 4, 1999).

Thomas, Timothy. "Physical Review Online Archives (PROLA): An Image Archive for the Journal *Physical Review," D-lib magazine* (June 1998).
[http://www.dlib.org/dlib/june98/06thomas.html] (October 24, 1999). Mr. Thomas reports that "an electronic archive is by no means static. [It] requires constant modification to keep up with the current high rate of technical change."

Unsworth, John. "The Importance of Failure," *Journal of Electronic Publishing* 3:2 (December 1997). [http://www.press.umich.edu/jep/03-02/unsworth.html]
(October 24, 1999).

Waters, Donald J. *Electronic Technologies and Preservation.* Washington, DC: Commission on Preservation and Access, 1992.
[http://www.clir.org/pubs/ reports/waters/waters2.html] (October 24, 1999).

IV
Selection of Materials for Scanning

Diane Vogt-O'Connor

Choice is Trouble.
        — Old Dutch Proverb

Introduction

election involves choosing among a number of options using informed judgment and selection criteria. Good selection techniques ensure that resources are invested wisely in digitizing the most significant and useful collections at the lowest possible cost without placing the institution at legal or social risk. Poor selection leads to the digitization of materials that are unusable or of little value.

Selection is a familiar process for archivists, librarians, and curators who must:
- Appraise materials for acquisition
- Determine priority for salvage during an emergency or for conservation
- Select contents for exhibitions and publications.

During these tasks, staff makes decisions that significantly affect the life and accessibility of collection contents. When reviewing materials for appraisal, conservation priority, or exhibitions, staff considers such factors as:
- Appropriateness to the repository mission and collections focus
- Appropriateness to a broader focus, such as a consortia goal
- Value in comparison to other materials held by the organization
- Demand from audiences in comparison to other materials held by the organization
- Restrictions due to legal status of collections
- Availability for use due to housing in remote or cold storage, poor preservation condition, or an awkward size (*e.g.*, 40"x60" architectural drawings) or format (*e.g.*, glass plates or framed or matted items).

Selection for scanning takes these factors, as well as others discussed below, into account. The process for selection for digitization can be quite similar to selection for other purposes. This chapter proposes three phases.
- ***Nomination.*** Nomination involves broad participation of collection creators, donors, researchers, managers, documented groups, and others. Stakeholders

and staff nominate materials for inclusion or noninclusion, indicating why the materials should be selected or avoided.

- **Evaluation.** During evaluation, a Selection Committee reviews the nominations based on criteria and makes determinations about including or weeding out materials.
- **Prioritization.** During prioritization, the committee ranks the selected materials based upon their value, use, and risk so that materials are digitized in order of value to the repository.

Users of this three-stage process identify and weed out problematic materials, while selecting and prioritizing appropriate materials for digital work. This approach produces a smooth workflow regardless of the amount of available funding.

The Selection Process	Who does it?	When?
1. Nomination of Materials: A. Nomination of What to Digitize (Form A) B. Nomination of What Not to Digitize (Form B)	Collection Stakeholders and Staff	At the start
2. Evaluation of Nominated Materials: Review Selection, and Weeding of Materials from the Nominated Materials (Form C)	Selection Committee	During formal review
3. Prioritization of Remaining Materials: Ranking of Materials based on Value, Use, and Risk	Selection Committee	During formal review

Why Select for Scanning?

Many organizations may be tempted to "just digitize it all" because selection seems labor-intensive and expensive. Might not resources be better spent on digitizing more content? Several compelling reasons for selection indicate otherwise.

- **Web Access as Publication.** When mounted on the Web, digitized collections reach the world's largest and most diverse audience. The Web audience includes scholars, students, the general public, news reporters, donors, collection creators, filmmakers, publishers, and discipline specialists, as well as less desirable users, such as potential thieves, vandals, and intellectual property rights infringers. Once alerted to an organization's holdings, this audience is apt to demand high quality reproductions, publication permissions, and access to the originals. Collection security and manageable policies for duplication, publication, and access should be in place long before the enhanced collection visibility generates increased requests and visitation. Effective preplanning can mitigate the impact of increased requests for access, duplicates, and permissions to publish or exhibit digitized items.

- **_High Costs and Limited Budgets._** Most organizations lack the resources to digitize their entire holdings, however desirable this might be to enhance access. The initial costs of selection and digitization pale beside the costs of quality control, metadata production, and indexing/cataloging. When scanning the entire collection isn't affordable, selection becomes not only feasible but essential.

- **_The Digital Mortgage._** Digital files come with a mortgage. Each organization must budget to transfer old files to new formats as software and hardware change and electronic media reach the end of their relatively short life expectancies (Puglia, 1999). This budget funds not only a substantial initial investment in digitization but also a digital infrastructure including staff, contracts, equipment, and software. Since digital files are significantly more expensive to manage over time than paper files, organizations must identify and program for substantial resources for the management of the large bodies of digital files they have created (Lowry & Troll, 1996; Marcum, 1998). Program costs don't cease when the Web site appears.

- **_Legal Issues._** Organizations often lack the intellectual property rights and permissions to the materials they hold. Copyrights; privacy and publicity rights; and issues of obscenity, defamation, and legally protected location information (federally protected caves, sacred sites, wells, and archeological sites), if not dealt with properly, can lead to lawsuits and costly settlements. Digitization done without thoughtful selection may result in the creation of digital files that can't be effectively used due to legal restrictions (Smith Levine, 1995). Determining the legal status of candidate materials is a crucial step in any digital selection process. Permission-seeking for selected materials begins immediately after selection.

Providing broad access to sensitive materials on the Web without appropriate consultation with specialists, affiliated groups, and donors may result in damage to the original resources (if protected locations are divulged) or to the institution's relationship with its donor community. When selecting materials for Web access, careful and accurate cataloging and contextualization and consultation with the stakeholder group(s) are both wise policies and good manners. Publishing materials on the Web is not equivalent to providing access to the material for a few hundred people annually in a reading room but is closer in impact to a television documentary or newspaper coverage. If there are qualms about publishing something on the front page of a daily newspaper, then the materials should not be put on the Web.

- **_Stakeholder Concerns._** Publishing culturally or ethically sensitive materials on the Web may raise a firestorm of protest, even if the collections are not legally restricted. Exercise temperate judgement that balances the need to respect valid stakeholder concerns against a wish to avoid arbitrary censorship. Consult with stakeholders when digitizing the following types of materials:
  - _Cultural information_ that is normally limited to members of special groups or cultures, such as sacred ceremony, burial, sacred and/or subsistence food-gathering site locations, or similar knowledge that can lead to damage to the resources if widely published.

- *Donor-restricted materials,* such as a request to avoid data release for 25 years after the donor's death.
- **Documentation.** During selection, the committee determines if candidate materials are well documented in terms of individual captions or complete and accurate item-level catalog data. If not, the organization is committing itself to significant additional expense to research the materials, fact-check information obtained, and write appropriate accompanying descriptions that provide a clear and accurate context. In fact, the National Archives staff estimates that up to two-thirds of the actual cost of digitization during the first ten years of a digital project is the creation of metadata and quality control work (Puglia, 1998). Exhibit text is even more expensive, more closely resembling traditional book or exhibit preparation costs.
- **Institutional Credibility.** During selection, the committee checks the accuracy and authority of all information to be included with the electronic resources. The institution corrects inaccurate information to protect its credibility and reputation. Increasingly, audiences using the Web evaluate electronic resources for quality. Common criteria include the authority of an organization, the background and reputation of the individual creator, and the verifiable footnotes or citations included with the materials.

Statistical Sampling

Regardless of how systematic the selection process and how clearly defined the criteria, no two committees select materials in precisely the same way, as no two groups have the same experience, skills, training, and viewpoints. Some historians and scientists prefer to digitize a random percentage of collections, as this sample allows a statistical analysis of collections that is apt to more accurately reflect the full universe of materials. If a significant portion of the expected audience includes scholars who work with sampling techniques, consider incorporating sampling into the selection process.

Although less effective at preserving scholarly context and narrative flow, sampling can be:
- More objective
- More effective at presenting a cross-section of the whole corpus of materials
- Less driven by scholarly trends.

When factoring a statistical component into a digitization project, base sampling on a random number table. Use the random number table to select particular containers and items or combine sampling with a more traditional selection approach. For example, select 5% of a collection using sampling techniques to give researchers a flavor of the whole. Since probably 2/3rds of the sampled materials will be weeded out due to their condition, restrictions, or other concerns, select many more items than are actually required.

The Selection Committee

By its nature, selection is very knowledge- and skill-intensive. A single individual cannot master all the necessary knowledge of subject disciplines, law, conservation, education, technology, and so forth. Most well-managed organizations form Selection Committees to avoid making costly mistakes. Committee members, acting in concert, can evaluate candidate materials judiciously from a variety of viewpoints, disciplines, and perspectives.

Candidates for the Selection Committee include:
- Discipline specialists related to the themes being covered in the project
- Education specialists, appropriate to the level of the project audience
- Digitizing specialists such as photographic and digital laboratory staff
- Librarians, archivists, and curators
- Researchers experienced in working with online resources
- Conservators and preservation specialists
- Lawyers.

Even a large Selection Committee may need additional help. Therefore, a wise organization figures out how to tap the knowledge and abilities of the stakeholding communities during the nomination process. (Note: Particularly effective representatives of those communities can also be included on the Selection Committee.)

Stakeholders involved in nominations can include:
- Collection creators and donors who have in-depth knowledge of the resources to be digitized
- Institutional staff who manage the collection and know the history of usage of the originals and their cataloging and physical condition status
- Individuals and groups represented in the collections and their heirs and communities who can decipher hidden meanings and explain cultural concerns about collection access
- User communities of scholars, students, educators, filmmakers, reporters, and scholarly publishers who know the market, audience, and secondary users of the project files and can help plan for them
- Members of the general public who can articulate community concerns and standards about sharing local knowledge internationally
- The middle people, including digital publishers, online order fulfillment services, search engine and technology companies, public television stations, and *edutainment* companies that have developed innovative strategies for distributing files and leveraging content to obtain funding
- Professional colleagues, discipline specialists, and funders who know the content and the institution's role and goals.

> ## Why Involve Stakeholders in Nomination for Selection?
>
> If funded by public monies, the collection-holding repository is responsible to each of these groups for how the institution manages, preserves, and makes collections accessible. Private repositories that take no federal or state funds legally may be able to disregard some of these communities. However, ignoring a repository's stakeholder community during selection is profoundly unwise as it affects the institution's reputation and may affect future donations and community cooperation.

The Selection Process

Those involved in selection must familiarize themselves with the goals of the scanning project and discover how the project supports the organization's mission, collections focus, audience, and cooperative strategies. Earlier chapters discuss these important issues.

Pre-Selection Tasks

At the outset, Selection Committee members should meet with other organizations, consortiums, or groups that are managing digital projects. Obtain their project goals and plans. Ask for copies of their audience studies and evaluations. Investigate the selection criteria used by partners and cooperators (*e.g.,* Library of Congress National Digital Library Collection Evaluation Criteria). Examine other projects of the organization, such as exhibits, publications, and courses to determine if their goals and plans suggest a digital component. Building on the expertise of others will speed the development of strong and systematic internal guidelines, policies, and procedures.

Nomination

During the nomination phase, stakeholders and staff members will use forms A and B to nominate materials for evaluation by the Selection Committee. Staff — particularly librarians, archivists, and curators — should be involved in nominating related groups of materials for evaluation. When nominating materials, staff should consider the following questions:

- How much of the collection is well and accurately documented at the item level in reliable and complete indices and finding aids, and where are these well-documented items?
- How much of the collection is in stable or good condition, and where are these stable materials?
- What portion of the collection is standard and consistently sized, normal contrast, black-and-white and/or printed materials, and where do these materials fall? Note: Avoid oversized, unusual or varying format, long-tonal range, color, and handwritten materials for start-up projects.
- What materials are easy to provide to researchers because of their size, format, or viewing requirements (for example, an 8" by 10" typed document or high resolution and high contrast photographic print original, but not a circuit camera negative or microfilm), and where are they in the collection?
- What percentage of the materials does the institution have the copyrights to or licenses for, and where are the public domain materials?
- What percentage of the materials has no restrictions or sensitivities of any sort (such as privacy, publicity, defamation, obscenity, and sensitivity, or donor restrictions), and where is this unrestricted and nonsensitive material?
- What materials are of highest monetary value and well secured, and where are they in the collections?
- What materials are judged to be at highest risk and why, and where are they located in the collections? Of these, which are stable enough to be scanned without damage or which have already been well photographed?

- What materials are used most frequently, how are they used, and where are they located?
- What materials are unique to the institution, and where are they located?

As noted above, capturing a variety of viewpoints in nominations and deselection at this stage ensures a more balanced and equitable selection process that reflects the full range of user and scholarly interests. Encourage staff, researchers, scholars, committee members, and other stakeholders to use Forms A and B to nominate candidate materials or identify materials that shouldn't be digitized. The forms should be available in the research room for all interested parties who are familiar with the collections. However, inform nominators that the Selection Committee evaluates all nominations and deselection recommendations and makes the final decisions.

Evaluation

The Selection Committee will first compare the nomination (Form A) and deselection (Form B) forms to see if any materials appear on both. Mark any materials that were both nominated and recommended for deselection as requiring special attention. The committee works through the questions on Form C for each of the nominated groups of items. If the answer to any one of the questions on Form C becomes, "no, don't digitize," remove the candidate materials being considered until the problem can be resolved. Some materials may qualify for digitization later when certain conditions can be met — for example, when permission can be obtained from copyright holders, or when copyright protection lapses, or when models or interviewees provide releases. Keep a record of these candidates so that the Selection Committee can reconsider them in the future.

> **E**valuation criteria can be adapted to various institutional settings. The criteria used in this chapter are geared primarily for museum environments.

If the quantity of selected items is inadequate for the size of the planned project, consider adding a random sample of the collection, as noted above (*Statistical Sampling*). For example, if 4,000 items have been selected and there is funding for 5,000, use a random number table to select the final 1,000. Review sampled materials for legal, preservation, sensitivity and other problems just as for other materials. When sampling, select an extra quantity (three times the number needed) to allow for materials that will be weeded out.

Once the Selection Committee has completed this evaluation process all inappropriate materials should be weeded out, leaving only excellent candidates for digitization.

Sample
How to Evaluate Collections

Look at each group of nominated items and answer the questions on Form C.
Name: the Quonsethut Academy of Fine Arts in New York
Mission and Collections Focus: Serves Art Historians, Publishers, and Educators in the United States in documenting art history, with an emphasis on landscape architecture and sculpture in upstate New York.

After the nomination period is over, the Academy receives three digitization nominations. The chart below describes the collections and how they were evaluated using Form C. The Status line indicates whether the materials were nominated (Form A) or suggested for deselection (Form B).

Collections Description	Status	Evaluation Decisions
Collection 1: Historic Photographs of the New York Branch of the American Atheneum of Art, 1870-1956, including images by Julia Margaret Cameron, Ansel Adams, and Alfred Stieglitz that document the institutional history. No model releases and the institution holds no copyrights.	Nominated (Form A) by visiting photo historian and staff curators	**Selected:** Almost 90% of this collection fits the Academy Scope of Collections and Mission. Copyrights of most of the images have lapsed. Permissions will be sought from materials still under copyright protection. As models are no longer living, no model releases are necessary. No publicity rights, E-FOIA, or sensitivities, except for one nude, which won't be digitized. Images are authentic, have associational, evidential, and artifactual values and can be scanned accurately. Collection is well cataloged and can easily be well contextualized due to existing exhibit catalog. Will add value by making very valuable images accessible internationally in conjunction with searchable indices. May avoid digitizing deteriorating glass plates and platinum print components of collection. Originals are well secured and placed in cold storage. Although no one else has digitized these images yet, the Academy's Consortium is interested in sharing the costs since other consortia members have portions of this collection and they can be combined into a virtual museum online.

Collections Description	Status	Evaluation Decisions
Collection 2: Matias Martin Papers, 1890-1979, contains correspondence with major world poets and artists, including six letters (<2% of collection) to the Director of the Quonsethut and Academy of Fine Arts. Most of the pages are very brittle, and many letters done with iron gall ink, leading to rips and tears.	Suggested for deselection (Form B) by lawyers and conservators	**Deselected (Weeded Out):** The collection contains high quantities of materials with defamation issues relating to living private individuals. The Academy lacks copyrights, and permissions will be expensive and time consuming to obtain. Recommended for deselection by lawyers and conservators. Reconsider in future (around 2024, when copyrights lapse and poets included are no longer living), as the interest from scholars will be high. In the meantime, funding will be sought to stabilize the collection.
Collection 3: Sylvia Hands-off Collection, 1930-1990, contains the office and personal papers of first curator Hands-off, plus records of the first 50 exhibitions held at the Quonsethut Academy of Fine Arts, including significant scholarly documentation and interpretive notes on exhibition topics that relate to the organization's mission. Copyright restrictions on 50% of collection. The papers have active mold in about 35% of the collection, but the estate left funding for conservation treatment. Researchers other than staff have not used it.	Suggested for deselection by an heir, as is felt to cast a bad light on the family	**Selected with reservations,** to be digitized once the collection has been stabilized. Precisely fits the Academy's Mission and Scope of Collections. The stakeholder's deselection request is judged to be frivolous and can be renegotiated to address the issues. Most of the collection was done as work-for-hire according to the Academy lawyer, so Hands-off's letters are not covered by copyright. Permissions can be sought from correspondents. No privacy, publicity, E-FOIA, sensitivity issues. Materials have evidential, associational, and informational value, authenticity, and visual accuracy. Materials are well documented and contextualized and will add significant value to already digitized exhibition catalogs and collections documentation. Audience is largely art scholars. The technology will work well for these items. Slightly over a third of the collection will require stabilization and cleaning. All items will require item-level cataloging to make them accessible to the international art community. Materials are currently inaccessible and digitizing duplicates no effort elsewhere. This would not qualify as a cooperative project, although it would link to other collections-related work in the Academy itself.

Prioritization by Value, Use, and Risk

If there are too many materials to digitize, prioritize the remaining items by *value, use, and risk* (Vogt-O'Connor, 1995). These evaluation criteria have been used for several years by many organizations. The committee assigns values to materials and computes totals to assist in this final phase of selection. However, each of these factors must be determined in relationship to the organization's mission and collecting statement, not in isolation.

Value

Materials to be digitized must have one or more of the following values in relationship to the organization's approved scope of collection statement.

Informational value refers to the material's topical content in relation to the organization's scope of collection statement and mission.
- High-value collections offer significant information on the key people, places, events, objects, periods, activities, projects, and processes (both natural and cultural) reflected in the collecting statement, thematic framework (if the organization has one), and mission.
- Moderate-value collections tell something of the topics and themes (such as the "who, what, where, when, why, and how") reflected in the mission statement and collecting policy.
- Low-value collections provide little information about key factors reflected in the mission and collecting statement.

Administrative value refers to the material's functional usefulness to the creating organization on a regular basis, such as the need for architectural drawings for building renovations or vital records for operation purposes.
- High-value collections are constantly being used for organization management.
- Moderate-value collections are occasionally used.
- Low-value collections are rarely reviewed.

Artifactual value, as used by archivists, is the same as intrinsic value and refers to original materials that have value due to their nature.
- High-value materials include items in good condition that are rare or interesting objects of material culture. For example, high-value materials include well-composed visual materials, holographic letters with unusual letterheads, or unique diaries; documents in rare historic processes such as platinum prints; materials in unusual genres and formats such as psychic photos or half-plate daguerreotypes.
- Moderate-value materials are widely used processes, such as albumen photographic prints, library bound books, or typed letters, and formats, such as stereographs, that are in good condition.
- Low-value materials are items in poor condition or copies or duplicates.

Associational value refers to original materials that have a relationship to an eminent individual, place, event, or group, such as letters created, owned, or signed by Thomas Edison or photos taken by or of Civil War soldiers.

- High-value materials include such items as the personal papers of a notable individual or group, or those associated with a project like an archeological excavation.
- Moderate-value collections might contain some correspondence or portraits of a notable individual.
- Low-value materials include copies or duplicates.

Evidential value refers to the documents' ability to serve as legal or historical proof of an activity, event, or occupation.
- High-value materials are the originals in an unmodified form.
- Moderate-value collections might include some records of legal value, such as birth certificates or legal copies of land records.
- Low-value materials are modified records or copies.

Monetary value refers to the current market value of an item. This value may change daily.

How to Score Value
When prioritizing different groups of materials, such as several manuscript collections or series within a single archival collection, or major donations:
- Score 6 points if a group of objects has high value in any of the above categories for a significant portion of a collection, *i.e.,* 10% or more (high value).
- Score 3 points if a group of materials has less than 10% or no high-value materials, but does have a moderate value in any of the above categories (moderate value).
- Score 1 point if the collection has no high or moderate value (low value).

Risk
Risk comes in several forms: legal, social, and preservation. Since legal and social risk will be weeded out during the selection process, this prioritization focuses on preservation.
- *High Risk.* The highest risk materials are primarily chemically unstable, which results in their self-destructing and damaging or contaminating nearby materials, as well as posing health hazards to staff and researchers who use them. Classic examples of high-risk materials are cellulose nitrate negatives and film and materials with biological or chemical contamination, such as mold, insect, and vermin that pose risks of information loss and health hazards. Examples of health and safety risks include materials contaminated with asbestos, Aspergillum mold, and Hantavirus. Other high-risk materials may be self-destructing due to inherent fault (such as iron gall ink, leather bindings with red rot, very acidic and brittle paper, and cellulose acetate film) and those items that may be causing damage to nearby materials (such as materials that have oozing tape).
- *Moderate Risk.* Moderate-risk materials are experiencing primarily mechanical or physical damage due to their housing and handling and the characteristics of their material (*e.g.,* folding strength). Materials that are deteriorating and losing their informational content naturally or gradually due to their

component processes and materials are moderate risks. Some examples include electronic and digital data carriers such as CD-ROMs and diskettes; most color slides, negatives, and prints and cellulose-ester based materials (acetate, diacetate, and triacetate); all flaking, retouched, friable, or handcolored images; letterpress books, particularly those with copy pencil inks; carbon copy correspondence; and some tracing paper drawings. Other factors being equal, smaller format materials, such as microforms, should be given top priority as more information is being lost. Also included in the moderate risk category, but of lesser priority, are items with holes, cracks, broken or ripped off pieces, rips, tears, punctures, losses, or those that are warped, folded, creased, wrinkled, cockled, buckled, scratched, abraded, stained, discolored, or otherwise structurally damaged or changing appearance (*e.g.*, color balance shift).

- *Low Risk.* Low-risk materials tend to be the more long-lived processes in undamaged condition and adequate storage conditions. Examples include items with freckle-like stains called foxing; dusty or dirty documents; and slightly faded blueprints and cyanotypes that are well housed in neutral pH materials. Some additional low-risk items might include visual materials that are separating from a mount or support and loose or friable media (such as easily smearable conte crayon, pastel, graphite, or charcoal) that are correctly housed.

How to Score Risk
When comparing groups of materials (for example, manuscript collections):
- Score six points if 10% or more of a collection is at high risk per the criteria above. Consider the entire collection as high risk.
- Score three points if less than 10% of the collection is high risk. Consider the entire collection as moderate risk.
- Score three points if there are no high-risk materials and 10% or more of the materials are at moderate risk. Consider the entire collection as moderate risk.
- Score one point if there are less than 1% high-risk materials in the collection and less than 10% moderate-risk materials. Consider the entire collection as low risk.

High-risk collections that are also high value merit digitization when the risk can be minimized or eliminated. The institution may choose not to digitize high-risk collections of low value.

Use
The third factor in determining a collection's priority for digitization is use. High-use materials are those that are requested most frequently for reference purposes by staff and/or outside researchers. If the digital project is geared toward a new audience, past use statistics will not be of much assistance. Determinations will need to be based on predictions of expected use. Talk to repositories experienced in working with the desired new audience, as well as to members of the audience when trying to predict usage. Consider a small pilot project to test audience response before committing to a major new initiative.

Generally, high-use materials have high value. On some occasions, materials of no perceivable value may suddenly become popular because of a particular charm of expression — for example, a turn-of-phrase in a letter, a quirky angle in a snapshot, or linkage to a previously uncelebrated event or activity. As scholarship changes, the values placed on materials also change. When high use can be predicted and risk minimized, digitizing is a wise access solution.

How to Score Use

Each repository must set its own values for this field based upon reference statistics and visitor logs. To do this, know the institution's usage statistics. Then establish median usage values for a collection. For example, if 10 were the median number of uses annually per collection, then a low use for a collection would be 1-6, moderate use would be 7-13, and high use would be 14-20+.

Putting it All Together: How to Score and Rank Collections

Value, risk, and use, when considered together and assigned scores (based upon numerical values of high=6, moderate=3, and low=1), indicate the collections requiring digitizing. The key is that each of these factors must be determined in relationship to the organization's mission and collecting statement, not in isolation.

After assigning numerical values to the ratings of value, risk, and use, the committee prioritizes the collections by their numerical scores. In the case of an identical score, compare the usage figures to determine which actually is higher. Also compare the actual types of deterioration to see which is the more threatening to the life of the collection.

In the example following there are two collections with a 15 score. Collection 5 has a larger scale problem with nitrate than Collection 1 has with mold; also the usage of Collection 5 was higher, making it the clear winner in terms of priorities.

Example of Ranking Based on Value, Use, and Risk

Name: the Quonsethut Academy of Fine Arts in New York
Mission and Collections Focus: Serves Art Historians, Publishers, and Educators in the United States in documenting art history, with an emphasis on landscape architecture and sculpture in upstate New York.

Collections Description	Value	Risk	Use	Score	Priority
Collection 1: Historic Photographs of the American Atheneum of Art, 1870-1956, including images by Julia Margaret Cameron, Ansel Adams, and Alfred Stieglitz that document the institutional history; some with mold (12%), and moderate (or 70) uses annually.	High (6)	High (6)	Moderate (3)	15	3 (has less use and risk than Collection #5)
Collection 2: Matin Femwit Papers, 1900-1989, contains correspondence with major world scientists in the fields of entomology, physics, and mammalogy and two letters (<1% of collection) to the Director of the Quonsethut Academy of Fine Arts. In good condition with a little foxing; relatively little usage as not yet cataloged. **Note:** Might be given higher priority if linked to a consortia need or outside funding priority that includes funding to do the work.	Low (1)- Does not fit mission or scope	Low (1)	Low (1)	3	5
Collection 3: Sylvia Hands-off Collection, 1930-1990, contains the office and personal papers of first curator Hands-off, plus records of the first 50 exhibitions held at the Quonsethut Academy of Fine Arts, including significant scholarly documentation and interpretive notes on exhibition topics that relate to the organization's mission. Copyright restrictions on 50% of collection. The papers have active mold in about 35% of the collection, but the estate left funding for conservation treatment. Researchers other than staff haven't used them.	High (6)	High (6)	Low (1)	7	4

Collections Description	Value	Risk	Use	Score	Priority
Collection 4: Quonsethut Academy of Fine Arts Oral History Collection, 1950-1999, includes oral and video histories, transcripts, and release forms documenting major artists, particularly sculptors and landscape architects of the American Northeast. Tapes have not been migrated or refreshed and many are on acetate bases or have flaking binder. Receives high usage, generally above 300 uses a year. Many requests for digital copies.	High (6)	High (6)	High (6)	18	1
Collection 5: Sculptor Tom McMakeitup, 1935-1999, includes the personal papers of New York sculptor and landscape architect Tom McMakeitup, a famed relativist. The collection contains his family, personal, and business papers, including correspondence, films and videotapes, and photographic documentation of his work for the RockePont-Mellon Family at the Kitchie Estate in the Adirondacks. The collection contains about 6,000 nitrate negatives; 4,000 feet of nitrate film; and about 5,000 color dye coupler slides on cellulose ester film. Usage is moderate among filmmakers, art historians, and landscape architects, with about 96 uses annually.	High (6)	High (6)	Moderate (3)	15	2 (Has more use and risk than Collection #1)

Summary of Key Points

The three stages for selection are:

1. Nominating materials for selection and deselection (stakeholders, the public, staff, and scholars);

2. Evaluating materials and weeding out materials that aren't appropriate for digitization using uniform deselection criteria (Selection Committee);

3. Prioritizing the remaining materials based upon the criteria of value, use, and risk to ensure that the most important materials are digitized first (Selection Committee).

Following this process ensures that the digital project is responsive to the individuals who will care about it most and have the biggest stake in its success. By thinking through major issues as materials are reviewed, the committee avoids potential problems from halting the project in mid-stream. Finally, thoughtful selection ensures that the organization spends its funding on the most important, useful, and at-risk items first, and that wise decisions are made.

Form A, Nomination Form for Selection

X Institution

Digital Project Nomination Form

1. Materials Being Nominated for Digitization (Please indicate collection number, series, number, box number, folder number, item control number or equivalent and the creator; caption of the item or a bibliographic citation to the fullest extent possible.) _____

_____

_____

_____

_____

_____

_____

_____

_____

2. Reason for Nomination (Describe why the materials are important, who might want to use them in a digital form, and what usages are likely if they are digitized.) _____

_____

_____

_____

_____

_____

_____

_____

_____

_____

_____

3. Potential Assistance Sources (Please indicate if you have any special knowledge or skills that might be shared with the X repository during the selection process. For example, can you provide caption information, historical background, or are you aware of potential funding sources or digital projects that are covering similar materials to those you are nominating?) _____

_____

_____

_____

_____

_____

_____

_____

_____

_____

4. Restrictions (Indicate if you are aware of any reason why the specified materials should not be digitized, such as legal, ethical, or cultural sensitivities. Please be as specific as possible citing a source, such as a law or culture group and a contact name if necessary.)_____

_____

_____

_____

_____

_____

_____

_____

5. Your Name: _____

6. Your Address: _____

7. Tel: _____ Fax: _____

8. E-Mail: _____

Note:
The Selection Committee will make all final decisions on what will or will not be included in the digital project. If you have any special information you would like to share with the committee, please write it below.

Form B, Nomination Form for Deselection

X Institution
Digital Project Deselection Form

1. Identify the Materials That Shouldn't be Digitized (Please indicate collection number, series, number, box number, folder number, item control number or equivalent, and the creator, or caption, of the item to the fullest extent possible.) __

_____
_____
_____
_____
_____
_____
_____

2. Reason for Deselection (Describe why the materials shouldn't be digitized or shared electronically. Identify problems or concerns that would arise, including legal, cultural, social, or ethical concerns. Identify who might be affected if the materials are available electronically.) _____

_____
_____
_____
_____
_____
_____
_____
_____
_____
_____
_____

3. Specific Restrictions (Indicate if you are aware of any reason why the materials should not be digitized by citing specific laws, policies, or equivalent documentation. Please be as specific as possible citing a source, such as a law or culture group, and a contact name if necessary.) _____

_____
_____
_____
_____
_____
_____
_____
_____
_____

4. Your Name: _____

5. Your Address: _____

6. Tel: _____ Fax: _____

7. E-Mail: _____

Note: The Selection Committee will make all final decisions on what will or will not be included in the digital project. If you have any special information you would like to share with the committee, please write it below.

Form C, Checklist for Evaluation

Answer each question yes or no.

Evaluation Factors:	Yes Digitize	No Don't Digitize
Mission Statement: Does the project fall within the repository or institution mission statement? If not, don't digitize.		
Scope of Collections Statement: Do the candidate materials fall within the repository's Scope of Collections Statement (Collecting Policy). If not, don't digitize unless the repository will redefine the policy to include the materials.		
Stakeholders' Deselection Requests: Has the repository received requests to select the materials for digitization from a stakeholder or reputable source? If so, are the requests challenged by equivalent requests not to digitize the materials? If so, don't digitize the materials. Note: If you have requests not to digitize that are judged frivolous or insubstantial by the Selection Committee, ignore them.		
Donor Restrictions: Is the candidate material unrestricted? If so, digitize. Has the donor or creator of the materials placed substantial and nonnegotiable restrictions on their usage that would prevent them from being digitized? If so, don't digitize the materials. Note: On occasion donor restrictions can be renegotiated.		
Copyrights: Is the material either in the public domain or covered by copyright protections that your organization has obtained? If so, digitize. If not, do you have reason to believe that you will be unable to obtain a license to use the materials? If yes, don't digitize until you have obtained copyrights or licenses/permissions.		
Privacy Rights: Does the material contain images of living individuals for which you have release forms (particularly for oral and video histories, medical records, personnel records, psychiatric counseling records, or photographs in which the individual is recognizable)? If yes, digitize. If no, do you have reason to believe you can't locate these individuals to obtain permissions or that they won't grant permissions? If yes, don't digitize unless and until you have the permissions.		

Evaluation Factors:	Yes Digitize	No Don't Digitize
Publicity Rights: Does your state have a publicity law (*e.g.,* California, Tennessee, New York)? If yes, does your material include images or recordings of famous individuals such as motion picture or recording stars, scientists, artists, or authors (living or dead)? If yes, do you have permissions or licenses to use the images from the individuals or their estates? If yes, digitize. If no, don't digitize until you have permission or licenses.		
E-FOIA and State and Local Equivalents: Are you required by law to digitize the candidate materials to meet the electronic Freedom of Information Act, the Paperwork Reduction Act, or similar initiatives? If so, digitize as long as there is no compelling reason why you may not digitize the items that can't be resolved at this time. If there is a compelling reason, don't digitize the materials.		
Sensitivity: Does the candidate material contain sensitive information (such as locations of sacred sites, burials, endangered species, fossils, threatened cultural resources [such as petroglyphs], or subsistence food gathering sites), or do the materials nominated present an unbalanced point of view or lack counterpoint perspectives? If so, are the project schedule and staffing adequate to seek consultations and permission-gathering activities from those groups affected and to consult with scholars of various viewpoints? If not, don't digitize the materials or digitize only materials that the committee is fully equipped to evaluate and put into context. Involve stakeholders on the Selection Committee or project staff.		
Evidential Value: Is the primary value of the materials evidential, or as legal or historical proof of an action or event? Does the material also have substantial informational and/or associational content of interest to a key audience? If so, digitize. If not, will translating the item from the analog realm to the digital realm so erode the value of the item that it will no longer serve its primary purpose? If so, or if the value is seriously eroded or there is no audience, don't digitize.		
Authenticity: Is the item to be digitized authentic and not faked, forged, or altered substantially? If so, digitize. If not, will digitizing the material lend a false authenticity to an inauthentic document or object? Is it impossible to correct the misconceptions through careful contextual documentation, captioning, and metadata? If so, don't digitize. Note: If the project involves substantial altering or retouching of a visual work for purposes other than parody or satire in potential violation of the Visual Artists' Rights Act, don't digitize the materials.		

Evaluation Factors:	Yes Digitize	No Don't Digitize
Visual Accuracy: Will the proposed scanning technique be able to capture the appearance of the item accurately? If so, digitize. If not, can the project move to a more sophisticated scanning technique such as color scanning to capture the information? If you can't capture the image accurately, don't digitize the materials.		
Documentation: Are the candidate materials well captioned? If so, digitize. If wrongly, poorly, or incompletely captioned, described, and labeled, are the project staffing and budget adequate to provide good documentation within the project timeline? If not, don't digitize the materials.		
Contextualization: Does the candidate material require substantial research and a sophisticated and expensive context in order to be useful? If so, can the project provide this context? If so, digitize. If not, will the ability to view the materials serially, but not side-by-side, decrease the value of the files to the audience significantly? If so, can the project provide a way to view materials side-by-side? If not, are there other items within the collection that can be selected instead on this topic? If the files are to be used, must a whole archaeological dig be reconstructed or must an archival finding aid be placed in the Encoded Archival Description (EAD) format or an equivalent effort? If so, are the project staffing and budget adequate to produce this contextualized treatment? If you can't provide the necessary context and the context is judged essential by the Selection Committee, don't digitize.		
Added Value: Are the candidate materials both valuable and available for the first time? If so, digitize. Does the project add value to candidate materials? If so, digitize. Does the project simply repeat work already in existence in an analog or paper publication (as shovelware)? If so, can the project be reworked so as to add value to the materials by improving access by creating: ■ new audiences for rare or unique materials currently accessible to only a few? ■ linkages to separated materials via HTML, SGML, or XML coding? ■ virtual collections of materials by the same creator; in the same process, media, technique, or format; or other linkage that are otherwise physically separated in real life on a single Web site or CD-ROM? ■ new indices and finding aids that are electronically searchable?		

IV. Selection of Materials for Scanning

Evaluation Factors:	Yes Digitize	No Don't Digitize
■ new searchability through post-scan processing via OCR or rekeying so textual files are fully searchable? ■ new ways to analyze the originals by techniques, such as microscopic scans, 3-D scans, or similar techniques? ■ usable files for research when the originals are too stained, deteriorated, or damaged for use by retouching or other treatment? If not, are the project staffing expertise and budget currently adequate to producing this new treatment of the material? If not, don't digitize the material until the digitization provides some added value.		
Audience: Is the expected new audience for the digital images the same as the existing audience for the originals? If so, will the repository consider recontextualizing the digital product to reach a broader audience? If so, digitize. Will the digital project help reach the same audience more effectively? If not, don't digitize the materials.		
Supplementary Selection Criteria: Has the audience set up supplementary evaluation criteria that must be factored into the evaluation process, such as the Teacher Usefulness Criteria developed for the Library of Congress? (EDC) Does this selection accommodate these additional criteria? If so, digitize; if not, don't digitize.		
Technology: Does the expected project audience require complex or sophisticated scanning techniques and viewing equipment to use the digitized images as envisioned? If so, is it likely that a sufficient percentage of the audience has this level of viewing technology? If not, replan the project. If so, will textual materials digitized require postscan processing, such as OCR processing or rekeying? Do images require retouching, very high resolution copying, color capture, or extensive coding to maintain linkages and hierarchies? If so, can the work be done within the project budget and timeline, using the project staff? If not, don't digitize.		
Condition: Are the candidate items either in stable condition or available as duplicates or copies for use in digitization? If so, digitize. If not, are the candidate items so deteriorated or at risk that it would be difficult or damaging to originals to digitize or copy them? For example, is there a need to disbind a unique scrapbook or rare book, remove items from frames and mats, or place pressure on a cockled and brittle image? If so, is stabilizing the originals too expensive and time consuming to do within the scope of the project budget and timeline? If so, don't digitize.		

Evaluation Factors:	Yes Digitize	No Don't Digitize
Control: Are the original items accessioned, described, and placed in secure storage? If so, digitize. If not, would digitizing them place the originals at risk by alerting potential thieves of valuable and vulnerable originals? If so, don't digitize.		
Duplication of Effort: Have you checked to see if the items have already been duplicated well elsewhere? If not well duplicated elsewhere, digitize. If digitized elsewhere, is the digital copy made of adequate quality? If so, obtain a copy from the other source and don't digitize the materials.		
Accessibility: Are the candidate items inaccessible, such as in cold storage? If so, digitize. If already easily accessible in multiple locations — such as through widely distributed microfilm copies or in many published exhibition catalogs — is there some special reason why digital copies are necessary? If not, don't digitize.		
Cooperative Project: Are the candidate items given priority due to some thematic, cooperative, or grant funding priority? If so, do these priorities fit the institutional mission and collecting statements? If so, digitize. If not, don't digitize.		
Cumulation: Is the candidate material a grouped and linked body of materials that draw additional value by being related to other materials held by the repository? Are they already digitized, already selected for digitization, or related to materials already well digitized by other organizations? If so digitize. If a single item and the effort are not for public relations alone or in response to E-FOIA, or are a request by a stakeholder, don't digitize.		

Sources

Atkinson, Ross. "Selection for Preservation: A Materialistic Approach." *Library Resources and Technical Services* 30 (October/December 1986): 344-53.

Bagnall, Roger S. and Carolyn L. Harris. "Involving Scholars in Preservation Decisions: The Case of Classicists." *The Journal of Academic Librarianship* 13:3 (1987).

Besser, Howard and Jennifer Trant. *Introduction to Imaging.* Santa Monica, CA: The Getty Art History Information Program, 1995.

Child, Margaret S. "Further Thoughts on Selection for Preservation: A Materialistic Approach." *Library Resources and Technical Services* 30 (October/December 1996): 354-62.

———. "Selection for Preservation" in *Advances in Preservation and Access.* Edited by Barbara Buckner Higginbotham and Mary E. Jackson. Westport, CT: Meckler Publishing, 1992.

Council on Library and Information Resources. *Scholarship, Instruction, and Libraries at the Turn of the Century: Results from Five Task Forces Appointed by the American Council of Learned Societies and the Council on Library and Information Resources.* Washington, DC: Council on Library and Information Resources, 1999.

DeStefano, Paula. "User-Based Selection for Preservation Microfilming." *College and Research Libraries,* September 1995.

Ellis, Judith, ed. *Keeping Archives,* 2nd edition. Melbourne, Australia: Thorpe and the Australian Society of Archivists, 1993.

Ester, Michael. *Digital Image Collections: Issues and Practice.* Washington, DC: Commission on Preservation and Access, 1996.

———. "Digital Images in the Context of Visual Collections and Scholarship." *Visual Resources* 10 (1994): 11-24.

———. "Image Quality and Viewer Perception." *Leonardo: Journal of the International Society for the Arts, Sciences, and Technology,* Supplemental Issues (1990): 51-63. Reprinted in *Visual Resources* 7:4 (1991): 327-52.

———. "Specifics of Imaging Practice." *Archives and Museum Informatics, Hands on Hypermedia and Interactivity in Museums.* Selected Papers from the Third International Conference (ICHIM/MCN95), San Diego, CA (October 1995): 147-58.

George, Gerald. *Difficult Choices: How Can Scholars Help Save Endangered Research Resources? A Report to the Commission on Preservation and Access.* Washington, DC: Commission on Preservation and Access, 1995.

Gertz, Janet. *Oversize Color Images Project, 1994-1995. Final Report on Phase I.* Washington, DC: Commission on Preservation and Access, 1995.

Gonzales, Pedro. *Computerization of the Archivo General de Indias: Strategies and Results.* Washington, DC: Council on Library and Information Resources, 1998.

Hazen, Dan, Jeffrey Horrell, and Jan Merrill-Oldham. *Selecting Research Collections for Digitization.* Washington, DC: Council on Library and Information Resources, 1998.

Kenney, Anne R. and Stephen Chapman. *Digital Imaging for Libraries and Archives.* Ithaca, NY: Department of Preservation and Conservation, Cornell University Library, 1996.

————. *Digital Resolution Requirements for Replacing Text-Based Materials: Methods for Benchmarking Image Quality.* Washington, DC: Commission on Preservation and Access, 1995.

Lesk, Michael. *Preservation of New Technology: A Report of the Technology Assessment Advisory Committee to the Commission on Preservation and Access.* Washington, DC: Commission on Preservation and Access, 1996.

Library of Congress National Digital Library Collection Evaluation Criteria prepared by EDC Center for Children and Technology, 96 Morton Street, 7th Floor, New York, NY 10014 (no date, 58 pages, plus bibliography and forms).

Lowry, Charles and Denise Troll. "The Virtual Library Project," in *Serials Librarian. ASIG Proceedings: Tradition, Technology, and Transformation Part I.* 28:1/2 (1996): 143-70.

McClung, Patricia A., ed. *RLG Digital Image Access Project.* Palo Alto, CA: Proceedings from an RLG Symposium held March 31 and April 1, 1995.

Marcum, Deanna. *CLIR Issues 2* (March/April 1998): 1-3.

National Research Council Committee of Preservation of Historical Records. *Preservation of Historical Records.* Washington, DC: National Academy Press, 1986.

Ostrow, Stephen E. *Digitizing Historical Pictorial Collections for the Internet.* Washington, DC: Council on Library and Information Resources, 1998.

Puglia, Steven. "Cost Benefit Analysis for Reformatting Options," Speech *Afterimages: Reformatting Visual Materials in a Digital World.* Offered by NEDCC and the National Park Service September 17, 1998, at National Archives and Records Administration, College Park, MD.

———. "Creating Permanent and Durable Information: Physical Media and Storage Requirements." *CRM* 22:2 (February 1999): 25-27. On the Web at http://www.cr.nps.gov/crm.

Smith, Abby. *Future of the Past: Preservation in American Research Libraries.* Washington, DC: Council on Library and Information Resources, 1999.

———. *Why Digitize?* Washington, DC: Council on Library and Information Resources, 1999.

Smith Levine, Melissa. "Electronic Publishing: A Legal and Practical Primer." *CRM* 18:9 (1995).

Vogt-O'Connor, Diane L. "Chapter 2: Legal Issues." *Museum Handbook, Part III: Access and Use.* Washington, DC: National Park Service and GPO, 1998.

———. "Is the Record of the 20th Century at Risk?" *CRM* 22:2 (February 1999): 21-25. On the Web at http://www.cr.nps.gov/crm.

———. "Preservation Reformatting: Selecting a Copy Technology." *Conserve O Gram* 19/11. Washington, DC: National Park Service and GPO, 1995.

———. "Reformatting for Preservation and Access: Prioritizing Materials for Duplication." *Conserve O Gram* 19/10. Washington, DC: National Park Service and GPO, 1995.

Vogt-O'Connor, Diane L., Virginia Kilby, and Joan Bacharach. "Chapter 1: Evaluating Museum Collections for Use." *Museum Handbook, Part III: Access and Use.* Washington, DC: National Park Service and GPO, 1998.

———. "Chapter 3: Publications" *Museum Handbook, Part III: Access and Use.* Washington, DC: National Park Service and GPO, 1998.

Waters, Donald J. "Archiving Digital Information" in *Tomorrow's Access—Today's Decisions: Ensuring Access to Today's Electronic Resources Tomorrow.* Proceedings of the Fourteenth Annual Conference of Research Library Directors. OCLC and the OCLC Research Libraries Advisory Committee, Dublin, OH: 1996.

————. *From Microfilm to Digital Imagery: On the Feasibility of a Project to Study the Means, Costs, and Benefits of Converting Large Quantities of Preserved Library Materials from Microfilm to Digital Images.* Washington, DC: Commission on Preservation and Access, 1996.

Waters, Donald J. and J. Garrett. *Preserving Digital Information: Final Report and Recommendations of the Task Force on Archiving Digital Information.* Washington, DC: Commission on Preservation and Access, 1996.

Weber, Harmut and Marianne Dorr. *Digitization as a Method of Preservation?* Washington, DC: Commission on Preservation and Access, 1997.

V
Overview of
Legal Issues for Digitization

Melissa Smith Levine
Legal Advisor, National Digital Library Project
Library of Congress

Introduction

This chapter provides an overview of basic copyright concepts and mentions a few of the legal issues to be considered in the course of a digitization project. It serves as a brief introduction to the range of issues that should be considered in any scanning or online project, including concerns that have surfaced as the National Digital Library Program has digitized and mounted selected Library of Congress collections for presentation on the Internet through American Memory. It is necessarily not comprehensive. The issues are complex. There is no simple recipe for identifying and resolving issues related to a particular collection. This discussion is not a substitute for competent legal advice.

In identifying these legal issues, this chapter pays special attention to the reasons for and concepts behind laws to help you recognize possible legal concerns and act responsibly in an arena that is still developing and often grey. Cultural and educational organizations are both creators and users of protected creative products. These organizations often are dependent upon or interwoven with artists, writers, and others who rely on their creative products for their sustenance. Thus, it is critical to take stewardship of intellectual property embodied in collections as seriously as the care of the physical collections. By understanding the legal concepts, you may be better able to apply them to digitizing projects. It is important to understand the reason and policies behind copyright laws in order to make reasonable assumptions about how to deal with making collections available on the Internet where the law is still rapidly evolving. Many of these concepts also will apply to other kinds of projects cultural organizations now routinely undertake to make their collections and activities more widely accessible. These include traditional print publications, licensing, television, radio, and video projects.

The focus here is on United States law and creative works protected under U.S. law. However, certain aspects of international legal concerns will be introduced. The presentation of material on the Internet is inherently international, so it is necessary to at least be aware of the larger context of global access and use of the materials you may make available online. Because so many participants in the School for Scanning courses have been employees of the U.S. federal government, a few concerns unique to federal projects will be raised for their information.

Copyright

Copyright in the U.S. is the exclusive right of authors in their original works. It exists from the moment of *fixation* in a tangible medium of expression (including software). It includes the right of the author to control the reproduction, copying, display, performance, and other uses of a work.

What Laws Govern Copyright?

In the United States of America, several bodies of law govern copyright. The first is the United States Constitution, Article 1, Section 8, which states: *The Congress shall have the power to promote the progress of science and the useful arts by securing for limited times to authors and inventors the exclusive right to their respective writings and discoveries.* This brief statement in brilliant simplicity implies that the underlying intention of the copyright provision is to move society forward by fostering creativity while also acknowledging the reality of human nature — that to encourage creators to share their works for the betterment of society, there needs to be a way to permit creators to profit from their work. James Madison described this concept of copyright in the Federalist Papers: *The public good fully coincides . . . with the claims of individuals.*

The Congress of the United States interprets the Constitution and produces law that is embodied in the United States Code. This is where you will find the current U.S. Copyright Act. The current act is only the latest of several earlier evolutions, each reflecting an attempt to address new technologies and new business models. For example, photography was not a protected medium until the 1870's, and movies were not protected until after the turn of the twentieth century. Since many projects address historical collections, you will need some basic familiarity with the current Copyright Act of 1976 as amended, as well as the earlier Copyright Act of 1909. Rules for calculating the duration of copyright differ, so you may have different results depending upon the nature of the material. Also, the event of *publication* (which is a term of art here) was of critical importance under the 1909 Act. Although still important under certain circumstances in the 1976 Act, the event of publication no longer determines the duration of copyright as it rigidly did under the earlier law. Publication and calculation of the duration of copyright are addressed below.

Another example of a law made by Congress is the Digital Millennium Copyright Act (DMCA) of 1998. This is a new law, which was made part of the existing Copyright Act in 1998. This extensive legislation continues to be widely discussed, and its far-reaching impact is still being assessed. The DMCA implemented certain international copyright treaty obligations of the United States in conjunction with treaties promulgated under the auspices of the World Intellectual Property Organization (WIPO). Other important areas addressed in the DMCA include:

- Limitations of certain liabilities of online service providers
- Exemption from copyright infringement for making a copy of a computer program if the copy is made for the purpose of maintenance or repair, and miscellaneous provisions regarding distance education
- Exceptions in the Copyright Act for nonprofit libraries and archives to make preservation copies of certain materials in digital form
- "Webcasting" of sound recordings on the Internet.

Many aspects of the DMCA may relate to projects undertaken by the educational and cultural communities. The U.S. Copyright Office prepared a useful summary of the DMCA, which is available on their Website at http://www.loc.gov/copyright. Look for it under the heading of *Legislation*. The U.S. Copyright Office was also charged with preparing a study on the impact of distance learning on copyright and the possible need for any new or special exemptions. This lengthy study is also available on their site at http://www.loc.gov/copyright/docs/de_rprt.pdf.

The next body of law to consider is case law. This is law created by judges as they interpret the application of the United States Code (and the Copyright Act embodied in the Code) and other laws to a particular set of facts brought before a court by litigants in a legal case. This chapter explores only a few examples, particularly in the area of fair use. Case law addresses applicability of law to a particular set of facts, so outcomes will differ depending on the facts. This is one reason that it is important to identify what you want to do and why and how you plan to do it. These are important steps in the planning process for legal documentation for projects.

Finally, international agreements and treaties such as the International Union for the Protection of Literary and Artistic Works (or the "Berne Convention") may need to be considered. The Berne Convention provides mutuality in copyright protection among member nations (those who have signed the treaty). The U.S. signed on in 1989, but Berne began much earlier in the 1890's. Generally speaking, nations tend not to join until they have a commercial interest in doing so. It was only when the movie and music industry pushed for the U.S. to join Berne in the interest of protecting U. S. works distributed or produced abroad that Congress had reason to seriously consider the matter. Similar commercial pressures in the international arena led to the implementation of the lengthening of copyright terms under U.S. law (to be addressed with copyright duration below).

At a very basic level, the Berne Convention provides mutual protection to member nations, also referred to as *national treatment*. In other words, member states must treat foreigners on at least the same terms as they treat their own nationals. When it comes to Internet distribution and access, it is in many respects unclear as to how to deal with questions of applicable law and jurisdiction. There is a slowly growing body of law in the U. S. as different states address analogous jurisdictional questions about which state's laws apply to a particular situation. The question of "whose law applies?" also is being explored in articles by law professors and experts. You also may hear about this issue in the area of taxation of transactions that occur over the Internet. It is an area to watch.

One item to mention in the context of the Berne Convention is the concept of moral rights, described in Article 2b of the treaty. Moral rights (or *droit moral*) protect certain ostensibly noncommercial interests of creators, primarily *attribution* and *integrity*. The right of attribution protects the creator by requiring that the creator be known or identified as the creator of the work, preventing others from being falsely named as the creator, and preventing the work of other people as being attributed to him or her. It has to do with the right to be associated with one's own creative product. The right of integrity prevents others from distorting, mutilating, or misrepresenting the creator's work in a manner that would affect his or her honor or reputation negatively. Generally, moral rights cannot be transferred — they are separate from economic rights and remain with the creator even after a work is sold.

This kind of right is not entirely consistent with traditional notions of property under U.S. law. Thus, in order to conform to the terms of Berne and permit the U. S. to sign the treaty, the U. S. pointed to other areas of U.S. law that provide analogous protections to creators, such as trademark, contract, and unfair competition laws. The U.S. Copyright Act was amended by Congress to include the Visual Artists Rights Act of 1990 as Section 106A (VARA). VARA applies only to a very limited category of creative works of art, including:

- Paintings, drawings, prints, and sculpture in a single copy or limited edition of 200 copies or fewer, if signed and numbered by the artist
- Still photographs if produced for exhibition purposes only and existing in a single copy signed by the artist or a limited edition of 200 or fewer signed and numbered by the artist.

Note that VARA does not apply to every kind of creative work. Excluded are such works as (but not limited to) posters, maps, globes, motion pictures or other audiovisual works, magazines, books, periodicals, newspapers, and advertising.

Moral rights under Berne and VARA are rights of the artist only — not the owner of the work if the work has been transferred or sold. In most European countries, moral rights cannot be transferred or assigned. In the U. S. this is true as well. However, in the U.S. an artist may waive his or her moral rights. This must be done in writing, stating the work and the uses to which the waiver applies. Note that moral rights under VARA do not appear to extend to electronic works.

The Copyright Act

As noted above, copyright in the U.S. is the exclusive right of authors in their original works. It exists from the moment of *fixation* in a tangible medium of expression (including software). It includes the right of the author to control the reproduction, display, performance, and other uses of a work. Note that "author" is the word used in the law to refer to any creator of a copyrightable work, regardless of whether the creator is an sculptor, painter, photographer, writer, or some other kind of creator. The Copyright Act protects these rights in a wide range of creative products including literary works; musical works including any accompanying works; dramatic works including any accompanying music; pantomimes and choreographic works; pictorial, graphic, and sculptural works; motion pictures and other audiovisual works; sound recordings; and architectural works.

The Act also protects the right of the author to create and control the creation of *derivative works.* A derivative work is a work based upon one or more preexisting works, such as a translation, musical arrangement, dramatization, fictionalization, motion picture version, sound recording, art reproduction, abridgment, condensation, or any other form in which a work may be recast, transformed, or adapted. A work consisting of editorial revisions, annotations, elaborations, or other modifications which, as a whole, represents an original work of authorship, is a derivative work.

This is a particularly important area to understand for digitization projects because many people believe that a digital copy of an existing work is a derivative work based on the existing item. This is also important in relation to the concept of *originality.* A work is only subject to copyright protection if it is sufficiently original, and there is some question as to whether a copy (digital or otherwise) of a work already in the public domain (that is, without any copyright protection) is a separately protectible work. One court in New York, in the case *Corel v. Bridgeman Art Library,* has held that there can be no new protection in such a copy. You can see how the conceptual line may be a bit blurry for some people in determining the difference between protectible derivative works controlled by a copyright owner and copies of public domain works in new media. Many cultural organizations and businesses confuse these concepts and rely on sometimes inaccurate conclusions in creating products and reproductions to generate revenues.

To Keep in Mind

In the area of copyright, it is important to keep the following points in mind:
- Copyright protects the actual expression of an idea, not the idea itself.
- Copyright notice (that is, the "c" in a circle or the word "Copyright" or "Copr." with the date of copyright and the name of the copyright owner) and registration are no longer required, since the U.S. joined the Berne Convention in 1989. Still, these notices are critical for determining whether an older work may still be subject to copyright. Under previous laws, publication without notice inserted a work into the public domain. It is still beneficial to register

new works so that people who may be interested in licensing can find the copyright owner and because registration with the U.S. Copyright Office is required to bring suit for copyright infringement and to obtain statutory damages for infringement.

- The absence of notice does not mean absence of copyright protection, particularly for newer works and for unpublished works (even older ones).
- Possession or ownership of a physical item does not mean the possessor or owner of the physical work owns the copyright.

Exceptions to Copyright

Copyright does not apply to all works, and it does not last forever. It is intended as a limited monopoly permitting authors to profit from their creative efforts and, eventually, for the public to be able to freely use creative works with the idea that such fluid use will inspire new creation benefiting society at large. When a creative work is not subject to copyright protection, it is referred to as "being in the public domain."

Works created by employees of the U. S. government in the scope of their employment are in the public domain under the U.S. Copyright Act. This is a matter of public policy, on the theory that citizens already have paid for this work with their tax dollars. This assumption applies neither to the works of state employees in the U.S. (states may and often do assert copyright in the works of their employees) nor to the works of employees of other nations.

The duration of copyright in the U. S. may differ depending on whether a work was subject to the 1909 Act or to the 1976 Act as amended. Keep in mind that there are grandfathering provisions in the 1976 Act as amended that may apply to earlier works. Generally, under the 1909 Act, works were protected for up to two 28-year terms for a total of 56 possible years of protection. Under the Copyright Act of 1976 as amended by the Sonny Bono Term Extension Act effective October 1998, works are protected for a term of the life of the author plus 70 years. For joint works (those created by two or more authors), duration is 70 years after the death of the last surviving author. For anonymous works, pseudonymous works, and works for hire, duration is the lesser of 75 years from publication or 100 years from creation.

Note that a *work for hire* is a work created by an employee within the scope of his or her employment. Copyright in works by independent contractors is assumed to lie with the creator — that is, the independent contractor. The works are specifically assumed not to be works for hire unless there is an agreement in writing to the contrary signed by the independent contractor prior to the start of work. If you are hiring someone to write a report or produce a creative product for your organization, and if you want the organization to retain the copyrights in the work produced by the contractor, it is critical to enter into a written agreement signed by the contractor before the commencement of work, stating the status of the work for copyright ownership purposes. Many contractors will refuse to sign something like this, so you may have to work out other ways to accomplish your goals, like obtaining some form of a license that allows you to achieve your goals while leaving the contractor some leeway to make other use of the work product. However, if he or she is producing something of a confidential nature, you should make every effort to clearly obtain all rights or otherwise address the matter in writing before work begins.

The following chart provides a helpful rule of thumb approach to calculating duration of copyright in the U.S. Keep in mind that this chart is less applicable to sound recordings and audiovisual works.

WHEN WORKS PASS INTO THE PUBLIC DOMAIN
Includes material from new Term Extension Act, PL 105-298

DATE OF WORK	PROTECTED FROM	TERM
Created 1-1-78 or after	When work is fixed in tangible medium of expression	Life + 70 years[1] (or if work is of corporate authorship, the shorter of 95 years from publication, or 120 years from creation)[2]
Published before 1923	In public domain	None
Published from 1923 - 63	When published with notice[3]	28 years + could be renewed for 47 years, now extended by 20 years for a total renewal of 67 years. If not so renewed, now in public domain
Published from 1964 - 77	When published with notice	28 years for first term; now automatic extension of 67 years for second term
Created before 1-1-78 but not published	1-1-78, the effective date of the 1976 Act which eliminated common law copyright	Life + 70 years or 12-31-2002, whichever is greater
Created before 1-1-78 but published between then and 12-31-2002	1-1-78, the effective date of the 1976 Act which eliminated common law copyright	Life + 70 years or 12-31-2047 whichever is greater

1 Term of joint works is measured by life of the longest-lived author.
2 Works for hire, anonymous, and pseudonymous works also have this term. 17 U.S.C. § 302(c).
3 Under the 1909 Act, works published without notice went into the public domain upon publication. Works published without notice between 1-1-78 and 3-1-89, effective date of the Berne Convention Implementation Act, retained copyright only if, *e.g.*, registration was made within five years. 17 U.S.C. § 405.

Notes courtesy of Professor Tom Field, Franklin Pierce Law Center
Lolly Gassaway

V. Overview of Legal Issues for Digitization

Note that "publication" is mentioned in this chart. As noted above, publication is a term of art that is defined in the Copyright Act. It generally refers to a sale or transfer of a work or a copy of a work, but it is not always a straightforward calculation. For example, the performance of a play is not a "publication" of a play for copyright purposes. Martin Luther King Jr.'s "I have a dream" speech was deemed by a court not to be a "publication" despite the attendance of thousands of people, the invitation of the press, and distribution of copies of the speech to members of the press. Use the chart as a rule of thumb, but keep in mind that publication can be a challenging concept that may require you to obtain legal assistance in some cases.

What is Fair Use?

Fair use is a concept unique to U.S. law that provides a defense to copyright infringement in certain special situations. If a use is a fair use, then one may copy an otherwise protected work without permission from the copyright owner and without the use being deemed an infringement. Other countries have a similar concept often called "fair dealing," but this is generally more restrictive and laden with administrative requirements. Fair use developed under U.S. case law (judge-made law) as an equitable way of dealing with certain kinds of copying that, under specific circumstances, were deemed excusable for reasons of public policy. Fair use existed only in case law until it was written into the Copyright Act of 1976, which distills these concepts of fair use that evolved in a long line of cases into a rather short statement that still leaves a great deal to interpretation in each situation.

Fair use is an exception to exclusive rights of copyright owners, and it is only available for limited uses for such purposes as criticism, comment, news reporting, teaching (including multiple copies for classroom use), scholarship, or research. Depending upon the balance of the following four factors, copying for these purposes is not an infringement under U.S. law. The four-factor test requires an evaluation of each set of facts under a balance of all of the following considerations — none of which is dispositive on its own.

What is the purpose and character of the use? Is the use intended for commercial or noncommercial purposes? Does the use do something that is somehow *transformative* — that is, does it use or copy the work itself as a parody that inherently requires the use of the work in its entirety?

What is the nature of the work? Is it a work of fiction or nonfiction? Fiction tends to receive a higher level of protection as more "creative" and, thus, is less subject to fair use arguments than factual works.

What is the amount and substantiality of the work used in relation to the whole? Does the copying take one line of a haiku poem or a multivolume epic? Is the copy one of the last pages of a whodunit mystery that, while only a small portion of the work, may destroy a buyer's interest in purchasing the book since he or she knows the ending already? This brings us to the last and often (though not always) heavily weighted factor:

What is the effect of the use on the potential market for — or value of — the copyrighted work? Note that this focuses both on existing value and potential market for a work. Copyright owners are putting old works back into circulation in many creative ways using new technologies. Therefore, it is more complicated to argue that a book has no potential market value because it is out of print. This can be a difficult factor to overcome if you plan to make a digital copy of a protected work for presentation on the Internet under a fair use argument.

A few recent cases demonstrate the application of fair use, including some cases where the fact that the use was commercial in nature was found not to be dispositive. In other words, the use was found to be fair despite the commercial nature of the use. You may recall the 1994 Supreme Court case of *Campbell v. Acuff Rose Music, Inc.* in which the rap group 2LiveCrew was sued for using Roy Orbison's well-known song *Pretty Woman* without permission or payment of royalties. 2LiveCrew's use was found to be fair despite its commercial nature. The band's attorneys argued successfully that 2LiveCrew's version was not a copy *per se* but a parody that required taking the "heart of the work" to make its point. This is an example of a transformative use.

In the 1998 case, *Leibovitz v. Paramount Pictures Corporation,* a court found a fair use in another situation involving commercial use where, in order to make a parody, the heart of a work had to be used. The famous photograph of actress Demi Moore for the cover of *Vanity Fair* magazine depicting Ms. Moore late in pregnancy and posed in the nude was parodied in an advertisement for a *Naked Gun* comedy film. The male star of the film was posed to mimic Ms. Moore. The original image of Moore was very carefully copied in detail. The court evaluated the facts on all four factors. Here, the original work was copied in its entirety for a commercial purpose. Yet, fair use applied because for the purpose of the parody, the use went to the heart of the original — the copying was required in order to make the parody. The use was found to be transformative and fair despite the commercial nature of the use and the fact that no permission was requested or fee paid. Note that no license fee is required if fair use applies.

Situations where no fair use was found include reproduction of a copyrighted poster of a work of art for a mere few seconds in a television sitcom. The poster was visible in the background of the set in the 1997 case of *Ringgold v. Black Entertainment Television.* The artist who created and owned copyrights on the poster and the original work of art on which the poster was based brought a copyright infringement action against the producer and broadcaster of a television program. The poster was used as set decoration in a manner ultimately found to be significant for copyright purposes because the use was for the same decorative purpose for which the poster was sold. This weighed against the television producer on the fair use factor, addressing purpose and character of use. Further, the fair use factor addressing effect of the use on potential market for the artist's work weighed against the producer because the use was commercial and took the heart of the thing without being transformative. The producer used the entire work where the artist already had existing licensing profits, thus negatively affecting the artist's income by failing to obtain permission and pay a license fee. There was no parody. Note that the poster appeared onscreen for only a few seconds.

It is difficult to determine whether fair use will apply in many situations. It is a concept that developed primarily in application to text, making the four factors somewhat difficult to apply to photos, artworks, and other nontext material.

Other Considerations

Copyright is in the limelight as the biggest concern for digitization projects, but there are other legal concepts that require attention. Brief descriptions of a few of these concepts follow.

Right of Publicity

The right of publicity generally is associated with public figures, frequently though not always celebrities and entertainers. Publicity rights address commercial gain in one's name, likeness, voice, persona, or other commercially exploited aspects of personality. Applicable laws vary state by state. Unlike copyright law, there is no federal law for publicity rights. This makes it difficult to determine what law applies to a particular situation. Further complicating matters is that in some states this right may continue after death. In other states it ends at the death of the subject. Advertisements incorporating digitally remastered film of now-dead celebrities are becoming routine — from John Wayne selling beer, to Elvis Presley selling pizza, to Fred Astaire dancing with vacuum cleaners.

Although many states have laws related to publicity rights, if you are dealing with materials that raise publicity concerns and are associated particularly with Tennessee, California, or New York, take extra care, since these states have well-developed laws in this area. You can seek permission from persons who have publicity rights directly from them — more often from their agents or attorneys. Often, depending on the nature of the use, you may be able to get a license fee for free or at a nominal expense. Finding the right contact is primarily a matter of detective work. Because publicity rights address economic rights, you may be able to argue that you have not intruded on publicity rights if your use is strictly noncommercial. The extent of possible liability is unclear for posting such material on the Internet, and thereby contributing to someone else's illegal use. Warnings placed on your site that tell your audience that they may need to obtain proper rights may be prudent if others copy content from your site for their own commercial purposes, although such warnings will not insulate you from possible liability.

Right of Privacy

The right of privacy is often referred to as "the right to be let alone." Unlike publicity rights, this body of law usually relates to private citizens rather than celebrities, though there are significant exceptions. Also in contrast to publicity rights, privacy rights are noncommercial in nature and protect people from intrusion into their seclusion or private affairs, from public disclosure of private information, and from being presented in a false light. Take special care if you are dealing with materials that place or otherwise document private persons in embarrassing situations such as photographs of nude persons (where the person is identifiable). It may be inappropriate at least and illegal at worst to publish such materials on a publicly accessible Web site. If the materials are sufficiently intrusive or embarrassing, the likelihood of obtaining permission from the subject is slim. The right of privacy generally ends at the death of the subject.

Defamation: Libel and Slander

Defamation embodies both libel and slander. It involves the publication to a third party of false written materials (libel) or spoken remarks (slander) that hold living persons up to hatred, contempt, or ridicule. This area of law varies state by state. If you are dealing with materials about a deceased person, keep in mind that the right usually ends at death. You cannot defame the dead. As a practical matter, there may be alternative legal theories under which children or heirs may be able to base a suit, so think very carefully before placing materials on the Internet that may be defamatory. This issue might come up in digitizing projects that involve correspondence or administrative papers where negative remarks were made decades ago and where the writer did not expect such remarks would be made public.

Obscenity and Pornography

Obscenity and pornography are such complex and large areas of the law that it suffices here to merely note these issues. Be able to recognize these issues and address them as necessary. Red flags for digitization projects include nudity, especially involving children, and any depiction of minors engaged in sexually explicit conduct. There are ongoing efforts at state and federal levels to control pornographic material distributed on the Internet, particularly child pornography, as well as efforts to protect child users of the Internet from materials that are more appropriate for an adult audience. Early efforts have been found unconstitutional. For example, the Electronic Communications Decency Act and its progeny were found unconstitutional partly on the theory that controlling pornography as outlined in that law would theoretically protect children at the likely expense of the First Amendment rights of adults, and partly on the practical assumption that child users can be protected from access to pornography through the use of filtering software. It is important to follow legislative efforts in this area.

In all likelihood, the proper balance will eventually be struck between managing illegal content such as child pornography online and the First Amendment.

Sensitivity to Content
Strictly speaking, this may not always be an area of legal concern, but it should be flagged in any digitization project. If you are working with anthropological materials or materials that involve people photographed against their will or in exploitive situations such as prisoners of war, be sensitive to the context of how the material was collected. Determine whether it is appropriate to consult with the subjects or descendants if possible. For example, give special attention to materials involving Native Americans, their sacred objects, and ceremonies. Examine the context in which original material was collected and consider the manner in which you will present such content.

Freedom of Information Act
This is an area of concern for projects produced by federal agencies of the U.S. government in particular. The Freedom of Information Act requires that the government provide public access to certain records, mostly involving governmental administration and policy matters such as organizational descriptions or procedures. Web sites are cost-effective tools to provide access to commonly requested materials that you may be legally required to make available to the public. A caveat: Some materials are specifically exempted from access, such as those whose disclosure might constitute an unwarranted invasion of privacy (*e.g.*, personnel, medical records), certain matters of national defense and foreign policy, trade secrets, privileged or confidential commercial or financial information, and certain law enforcement records.

Linking
A handful of cases have been brought in recent years involving linking between Web sites. One of the more publicized of these cases involved Ticketmaster and Microsoft. Microsoft linked to an area of Ticketmaster's Web site "past" the home page. Anyone accessing Ticketmaster's site via the subject link from Microsoft would bypass the advertising on Ticketmaster's home page. Ticketmaster argued that this would ultimately deprive it of advertising revenues while Microsoft argued, among other things, that the link actually created greater exposure for Ticketmaster's products and would increase Ticketmaster's sales. This case was settled.

More recently, the Church of Jesus Christ Latter-Day Saints sued the Utah Lighthouse Ministry in a federal district court in Utah for linking to Web sites that contained copyrighted works of the Church of Jesus Christ Latter-Day Saints without its permission. In December 1999 the court issued a preliminary injunction preventing the Utah Lighthouse Ministry from providing these links. This case raises the question of *contributory infringement*. Under this case, if you link to sites that contain material that infringes on a copyright, you may be held liable for copyright infringement even if you did not post ("copy") the material yourself. This case has chilling ramifications for the fluidity of the

Internet as well as First Amendment implications. Monitor this case for consideration in planning your Web site — a search of the parties' names on any search engine will provide references.

It has become common practice to obtain permission to link to other sites — or to at least notify the subject site. This is particularly true for commercial sites. This is a conservative approach, and by no means a requirement at this time. Like so many other issues, the consideration of the context of the link is important. By analogy, one would not request permission to list a work in a bibliography. If you are creating a resource list on a noncommercial, educational site, this concern is probably limited. Tread with caution if you are linking in a manner that implies some kind of endorsement or otherwise might trigger a right such as trademark or unfair competition. The existence and extent of liability in this area are unclear to date.

How to Proceed

One theme of this discussion is the evolving nature of the legal environment as new factual situations arise *vis à vis* the Internet. The first step in forging ahead in this changing scene is to educate yourself. Get a sense of the issues; this article is intended as a starting point. Once you have some familiarity with the legal as well as financial and administrative concerns, it is advisable to establish within the organization some policy framework so it can develop consistent practices and ways of approaching projects.

Each project should include for internal use and communication a description of the material selected for digitization. What is it, where is it from, how and why was it selected for digitization? Is the material of extraordinary interest? Is donor enthusiasm driving the project? Is the original material to be conserved in the process or is this a project where the materials will be destroyed in the course of the effort, as in so-called "brittle book" projects? Determining the provenance of the original material is the critical first step in a legal evaluation of the rights status of the subject materials. What were the terms of transfer — was the material given to or purchased by your organization? Were there any written terms, such as a deed of gift or a will? If so, get a copy and read it carefully. You may need the assistance of an attorney to interpret the terms.

You should then be able to determine whether you will need to pursue permissions to reproduce the selected content on a Web site. Keep in mind that the legal status of the original material is a significant factor in any selection process. If you have exciting materials that are heavily encumbered by the need to go through an onerous permissions process, you may determine that on balance it is more expeditious to consider another body of material. Otherwise, factor in the cost of permissions, including the administrative expense (staff time, reference resources, telephone calls, faxes, mailing...).

In planning a project, have a clear sense of your institution's purpose. Budget time and resources accordingly. Digitization projects tend to be labor intensive — this is not merely the technical equivalent of photocopying! Staff and contractor time are costly and tend to be underestimated. Decide as a practical matter whether you are willing and able to pay permission fees if necessary. Develop form permission letters to minimize your administrative efforts. You may as a policy matter prefer not to include any materials encumbered by rights. Consider how you expect people to use the Web offerings and plan around that expectation. Document your efforts. Plan to include notice statements online with each project including information about permissions obtained and contacts for those rights holders ("legal metadata"). They should be incorporated into the graphic design in a consistent way so that users know where to find rights information in a predictable way. Keep in mind that individuals who grant permission for use, in contrast to businesses, may prefer that you not place their home address on your Web site for privacy reasons. Thus you may need to serve as the contact point to refer permission requests from third parties who wish to use materials posted on your site with permission — another administrative consideration.

You may wish to look at the notice statements provided in the American Memory home page as a starting point. Note that there is a statement for American Memory overall and a statement tailored to each collection presented on the respective collections' home pages. Your notices should be tailored to your project, your organization, and other particulars unique to your efforts. Notice statements provide important information to users of your site, although it is unclear as to what extent notices will insulate you from certain liabilities. In contrast to the American Memory notices, many Web sites incorporate very legalistic notices. The tone and content will vary depending upon your project, the comfort level of your organization, and any legal advice you may obtain.

Sample American Memory Notice Statements

General Statement
http://lcweb2.loc.gov/ammem/copyrit2.html

Gottscho-Schliesner (commercial rights reserved)
http://lcweb2.loc.gov/ammem/gschtml/gottres.html

Conservation Collection (mixed-media collection)
http://lcweb2.loc.gov/ammem/amrvhtml/consres.html

Words and Deeds (items made available with permission)
http://memory.loc.gov/ammem/mcchtml/corres.html

References for Information About Law and the Online World

The "law of cyberspace" evolves daily as new technologies emerge, new legal analogies develop, and as the courts and Congress respond with new opinions and laws. By the time you read this document, new materials will be online. As a practical matter, many sites are updated or changed frequently. Some addresses may disappear altogether. Note that quoted material refers to text from the described site.

Part of the excitement of using online resources is that you never know what you may find. Each site is likely to link to other interesting information. Some of the addresses listed here, like the Copyright Office's site, provide solid resources that you will refer to over and over again. Some provide legislative updates, like the Library of Congress' **THOMAS** site. Other addresses are policy oriented and contain think pieces and commentary about legal developments related to cyberspace. This list is not an endorsement of any particular site or point of view expressed. There is a phenomenal amount of material being generated on this subject both in print and electronic form — this list is by no means exhaustive. It is a starting point for information about legal issues related to using and participating in the Internet.

I encourage you to look around and educate yourselves — both about the actual state of the law and the range of opinions that form the debates about the legal future of the Internet. These debates only begin with questions about copyright. Try to keep up with the ongoing debates to obtain a general understanding of the concepts behind existing laws. Then apply common sense to your day-to-day work. Ideally, you will have an attorney at your disposal who can assist you. Coordinate your activities with your General Counsel's Office, if applicable. There is no substitute for qualified legal counsel.

Start with **The Library of Congress** home page at:
> **http://www.loc.gov/**

It will take you to the **National Digital Library Project/American Memory Collection.** Look at that for examples of restriction and notice statements. Look at other sites — commercial, nonprofit, and government — to see how different organizations handle these issues.

Also from the Library of Congress' home page, see **The Copyright Office's** site. This provides a plethora of information about copyright. Information about copyright basics is a must. Also see online the Copyright Office's indispensable circulars describing in simple terms the practical aspects and applications of copyright law — there are also instructions for how to obtain a free set of print copies of the circulars. This site is indispensable for text of the copyright law, international conventions, and legislative updates. Note the information about CORDS (The Copyright Office Electronic Registration, Recordation and Deposit

System), an exciting project in the works for online, digital registration and deposit of works for copyright purposes.

The Library of Congress' home page also contains **THOMAS.** Named for Thomas Jefferson, whose personal library formed the core of the Library of Congress, THOMAS provides regularly updated information about legislation of the U.S. Congress. Be on the lookout for legislation about copyright, privacy, and obscenity/pornography matters (to name a few) as they relate to the Internet.

The **Cyberspace Law Institute** (CLI) seeks to, "study, and help to develop, the new forms of law-making required by the growth of global communications networks and online communities." There is plenty of information geared for non-lawyers; find the link to **Email Course on Cyberspace Law for Non-Lawyers.** This virtual course will be over by the time you read this, but the lessons should be archived on the CLI site. This articulate presentation may be found at:

> **http://www.cli.org**

The **UVa Copyright Resources** from the University of Virginia provides general copyright information; policy statements regarding copyright matters such as the ownership of works produced by University of Virginia's faculty and students; and guidance for permission letters. Find it at:

> **http://wwwllib.virginia.edu/dmmc/copyright/local.html**

When Works Pass Into the Public Domain is a handy chart by Laura N. Gassaway, Director of the Law Library & Professor of Law, University of North Carolina, Chapel Hill. The chart, reproduced in this chapter, helps to determine the duration for many copyrighted works where the facts are fairly straightforward; it is less helpful in more complex situations.

> **http://www.smartbiz.com/sbs/arts/ipi5.htm**

The chart was obtained from a link from the **U.S. Intellectual Property Information** site. See it at:

> **http://www.fplc.edu/tfield/order.htm**

The **Legal Information Institute, Cornell Law School** provides copies of recent Supreme Court decisions, the United States Code (laws promulgated by the U.S. Congress), historic decisions, and more. It is a bit legalistic but is a complete and quite useful resource. See the area called **material organized by legal topic.** Then click on **intellectual property.** Then click on **copyright** or **right of Publicity/Right of Privacy.** Start at:

> **http://www.law.cornell.edu/lii.table.html**

The **Guide to Copyright Bibliography** is a list of handy sources, mostly law review articles. Some are accessible for nonlawyers. Peruse the list and see what looks helpful:

> **http://www.music.indiana.edu/tech_s/mla/legcom/bib.htm**

The **International Federation of Library Associations (IFLA)** home page is at:
> **http://www.nlc-bnc.ca/ifla/home.htm**

It contains useful items, including a bibliography of relevant articles, journals, organizations, companies, and online collections. It also includes examples of copyright policies and international treaties available through the IFLA site or directly at:
> **http://www.nlc-bnc.ca/ifla/ll/cpyright.htm**

The **American Library Association's** site provides information on legislative developments that affect libraries; copyright also continues to be a significant concern. From their home page, look at their sections, **Copyright and Intellectual Property** and **Intellectual Freedom**. They also have a listserv — get instructions on how to subscribe at their home page at:
> **http://www.ala.org/alawashington.html**

The **Coalition for Networked Information** (CNI) has a **Copyright and Intellectual Property Forum** listserv intended to "give those who ask, answer, and discuss copyright questions of any type a forum for discussion...not limited to any one area such as copyright for electronic materials." Their archive is at: **ftp://ftp.cni.org/CNI/forums/cni-copyright.** Better yet, subscribe by sending an e-mail note to the Coalition ListProcessor (LISTPROC@CNI.ORG) with the following message:
> **subscribe CNI-COPYRIGHT <your real name>**

The **Sixth Conference on Computers, Freedom, and Privacy at the Massachusetts Institute of Technology, March 27-30, 1996** addressed a wide range of issues in the context of the Internet including copyright, privacy, and freedom of expression. It includes links to content from discussions by distinguished panelists. This will help to give you a sense of the range of issues:
> **http://swissnet.ai.mit.edu/ switz/cfp96/index.html**

The **Journal of Online Law** (JOL), "is an electronic publication of scholarly essays about law and online communications — law and cyberspace." These well-written essays are useful for both lawyers and nonlawyers. Find the JOL at:
> **http://www.wm.edu/law/publications/jol**

A License to Copy describes a proposal to set up a licensing scheme for academic institutions based on the number of enrolled students for certain uses of certain copyrighted materials. The framework is similar to the accepted licensing practices of the music industry handled by ASCAP and BMI. Proponents say it would ease the burden of tracking down and paying permissions for higher education. Opponents say it erodes fair use:
> **http://www.copyright.com/chronicl.html**

The **Electronic Frontier Foundation** is "a non-profit civil liberties organization working in the public interest to protect privacy, free expression, and access to public resources and information in new media." Find legislative information and more at:

http://www.eff.org/

The **Digital Future Coalition** includes copyright and information about other legal issues as they relate to the Internet. The DFC was formed in the fall of 1995 "to work towards a thorough, broad and balanced congressional debate of U.S. copyright law and policy." See their list of member organizations, which links to other useful sites:

http://www.dfc.org/

An interesting article by David Post, Visiting Associate Professor of Law, Georgetown University Law Center, is **The State of Nature and the First Internet War: Scientology, Its Critics, Anarchy and Law in Cyberspace** at:

http://www.reasonmag.com/reason/9604/Fe.POST.text.html

Another article by Ann Okerson of Yale University, **Who Owns Digital Works,** is accessible and sets forth many of the challenges for applying copyright to online activities. The print version is in *Scientific American,* July 1995, page 80. Find it online at:

http://www.sciam.com/WEB/0796issue/0796okerson.html

Sources

Nicholas Negroponte. *Being Digital.* New York: Knopf, 1995. An interesting think-piece about the big picture concepts associated with digital information. Helpful for those of us who are not technically inclined.

A Museum Guide to Copyright and Trademark (American Association of Museums) by Michael S. Shapiro and Brett I. Miller, Morgan, Lewis & Bockius, LLP. 1999. This book was supported with a grant from The Pew Charitable Trusts, with additional support from The J. Paul Getty Trust.

Lance Rose. *NetLaw: Your Rights in the Online World*, 1st ed. New York: Osbourne/McGraw-Hill,1995. An introduction to application of U.S. law to the online world. Minimal legalese useful for lawyers and nonlawyers.

VI
Technical Primer

Steven Puglia
National Archives and Records Administration

Introduction

This chapter exposes readers to the technical terminology and concepts of the digitization process. Specifically, it provides basic technical information related to digitizing library collections, archival holdings, and other materials from cultural institutions. As an overview, the chapter does not go into the technical detail needed to actually perform digitization. Instead, it is intended for those who manage activities or work on other aspects of digitizing projects. For some readers, this chapter may be a bit basic, for others a bit complex, but it tries to strike a reasonable balance that is helpful.

The Digital Image

Digitization converts an image into a series of picture elements or pixels, little squares that are either black or white (binary), a specific shade of gray (grayscale) or color. Each pixel is represented by a single or series of binary digits, either 1s or 0s. The pixels are arranged in a two-dimensional matrix called a bitmap. This

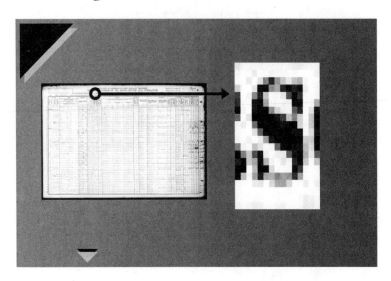

is referred to as a raster image. If you zoom in on a raster-based digital image, you will see the image is composed of a series of rows and columns of square pixels. A raster image is relatively analogous to traditional photographs, which are composed of image-forming grains or clumps of either silver or dyes. Where possible, this chapter compares aspects of digital technology to traditional photographic technology as a point of reference.

Vector image files are a different type of computer image distinct from raster images. Many computer programs (drawing, illustration, 3D modeling/rendering, computer-aided design/computer-aided manufacturing, and architectural design) use vectors — arrows of direction, points, and lines — that define shapes, as compared to the individual picture elements used to represent a raster image. This chapter will not discuss them further.

The Digitization Process

Digitization is the process of converting an analog signal into a digital signal, known as an A/D (analog to digital) conversion. For raster images, an analog voltage signal (from any of several types of imaging sensors), proportional to the amount of light reflected or transmitted by an item being digitized, is divided into discrete numeric values. The number of values is the bit depth for each pixel.

Common Digital Imaging Sensors (image detectors)

One important part of digitizing is the type of imaging sensor used. These image detectors can be compared to the film used in photography. The common digital imaging sensors are:

- CCD: Charged coupled devices, or CCDs, used in both flatbed scanners and digital cameras
- PMT: Photo-multiplier tubes, or PMTs, used in drum scanners
- CMOS: Complementary metal oxide semiconductors, or CMOS chips, used in low-end flatbed scanners and low-end digital cameras.

The most common sensor used in scanners is the charged-coupled device or CCD, used in all types of scanners and digital cameras. The photo multiplier tube, or PMT, is used only in drum scanners for the graphic arts or prepress market, *i.e.,* printing and publishing. More recently, complementary metal oxide semiconductor or CMOS sensors have been introduced as a low-cost alternative to CCDs. CMOS chips are manufactured in the same way as standard computer chips and are therefore less expensive to manufacture. Eventually, CMOS chips could replace the CCD as the predominant sensor in the marketplace, but currently, due to certain technical deficiencies, they do not produce the same image quality of CCDs and cannot match the resolution of CCDs. At this time, CMOS chips are used only in low-end digital cameras and scanners.

CCDs are produced in a variety of designs and shapes. A single row of CCD sensors (or photo diodes) arranged in a straight line are referred to as line arrays. Line arrays are used commonly in flatbed scanners. Area arrays comprise a two-dimensional set of rows and columns of light sensors. Area arrays are used commonly in digital cameras.

In both scanners and digital cameras, a lens or set of lenses are used to focus an image onto the sensor — a CCD, PMT, or CMOS chip. Sometimes people refer to digital imaging as lens-less. This is not true. Without a lens to focus the light, digital images would be blurry, just as in photography. All scanners have lenses. In most cases, the design of the scanner hides the lens(es) within the body of the scanner.

Scanners also have built-in light sources to illuminate the items being scanned. The light is either reflected (as with documents or photographic prints) or transmitted (as with microfilm, photographic negatives, or color transparencies) by the item being scanned, and the image is focussed by the lens(es) onto the imaging sensor. In the case of CCDs, the light falls onto the little light sensors or photo diodes on the CCD. These sites or diodes generate an electrical current, or voltage. The amount of voltage generated is proportional to the amount of light hitting the individual sensor. The brighter the light, the higher the voltage that is given off by the site on the CCD.

Analog to Digital Conversion

The analog electrical signal generated by the sensor is processed via the analog to digital conversion. The electrical signal generated at each light sensor or photo diode is divided into discrete numerical values that are proportional to the amount of light reflected from or transmitted by the item being scanned. The total number of discrete numerical values possible is determined by the sampling bit depth, while the specific numeric value for an individual pixel is based on the specific amount of light reflected or transmitted from that point on the original image.

Also, once a digital image has been created and stored in any media, there is a corresponding digital to analog conversion that allows the computer to present the image in a human readable form on either a display or printer. Displaying an image on a computer monitor or printing the image on a printer are both examples of an analog representation of a digital image.

Basic Image Measures

There are three important measures of every static digital image:

1. Resolution. The number of dots, or pixels (picture element), used to represent an image. This is always given as a measure of linear or area density (*e.g.*, 300 dots/inch).
2. Pixel Bit Depth. This measure defines the number of shades that can actually be represented by the amount of information saved for each pixel. These can

range from 1 bit/pixel for binary (fax type) images to 24 bits per pixel in high quality color images.

3. Color. There are many ways to represent, compress, and distribute color images. Suffice it to say that the smaller the image file size, the less accurately it renders the original image.

1. Resolution

Resolution, or spatial frequency, is the number of times an image is sampled during the scanning process. Resolution — the number of pixels in an image — can be described in a number of ways:

DPI— dots per inch
PPI— pixels per inch
LPI— lines per inch, used for halftones

The scanning resolution and the resolution of digital image files are most appropriately referred to as pixels per inch or PPI. Dots per inch or DPI is considered a printing term and is most appropriate when referring to the resolution at which a computer printer produces a print. However, DPI is a more generic term and is more commonly used than PPI. LPI is a term that refers to a half-tone screen value. A half-tone screen converts an image into a series of dots that can be reproduced on a computer printer or a printing press; continuous tone digital images are converted to half-tone images when they are printed on most types of computer printers, including ink-jet and laser printers. Some printers print continuous tone image and do not convert the image.

1.a. Pixel Array

The pixel array is the number of pixels across both dimensions of an image in terms of rows and columns across the dimensions of the image. As an example, an 8"x10" photograph is scanned at 300 ppi. This produces a file that has a pixel array of 2400 x 3000 pixels.

Generally, lines per inch (LPI) is a term used for halftones (for reproduction on a printing press) and is not used for continuous-tone images. However, "lines" or rows of pixels is a term used within the photographic industry as a common shorthand for the number of pixels across the long dimension of digital images of photographs. Since photographs come in many different formats and sizes (ranging from small negatives to large prints), it is hard to refer to pixels per inch (PPI) of resolution when producing digital images of the same size because the PPI will vary depending on the size of the photographic original.

An 8"x10" print scanned at 300 ppi produces a file that is 2400 x 3000 pixels.
A 4"x5" negative scanned at 600 ppi produces a file that is 2400 x 3000 pixels.
A 35mm negative scanned at 2100 ppi produces a file that is 2000 x 3000 pixels.

Each of these files is referred to as a 3000 line file, and all sizes are prior to applying any type of compression.

1.b. Resolution - True vs. Interpolated

Optical (true) resolution is the inherent resolution of the scanner based on the size of the imaging sensor and the magnification of the optical system. Interpolated resolution is synthetic or calculated resolution. Interpolation is a mathematical process that is used to increase or decrease the resolution of an image. This can be done during or after scanning. Higher optical (true) resolution in a scanner will provide better image quality than interpolated resolution. It is recommended that you obtain a scanner with as high an optical resolution as is affordable, not just in terms of the price of the scanner, but also in terms of the cost to store each image file.

> **... obtain a scanner with as high an optical resolution as is affordable**

Interpolation can be as simple as changing the optical resolution to a lower value for display purposes, or as complex as detecting and rescreening halftone areas of a document. Some interpolation algorithms work better than others. Generally, more expensive image processing software has better algorithms. However, there are exceptions because more and more of the interpolation algorithms are being built into the scanner hardware. Most interpolation algorithms represent a trade-off between image quality, speed, and image file size. It is highly recommended that you test the actual documents to be scanned with the actual scanners and image enhancement algorithms to be used. It is often a good idea to buy a more expensive scanner or to add an image processing software package — one that has better image processing algorithms. Even though most users may use only a small number of all the features available, high quality images will at one point or another need to be processed with image processing algorithms.

> **Test documents with the actual scanners to be used**

1.c. Digitizing Resolution

Digitizing resolution can be divided into two generic categories. Reproduction resolution is the resolution needed to provide a desired image quality for a specific type of output device. Preservation resolution is the level of resolution that reproduces all the information in the original image or document. Using photographs as an example, these levels could be:

- Reproduction—screen resolution, which is a minimum of 600 x 400 pixels, or print resolution, which is usually 300 dpi to 600 dpi.
- Preservation—match the original (examples for color negative or color transparency). This is a theoretical resolution limit based on the resolution and granularity of the original film and the resolution of the lens used to take the photograph. The actual desired digital resolution will vary depending on the photographic film (and the developer used), the original camera lens, the significant feature size that is desired to be reproduced, and the quality of the scanner used for digitizing.
  - 3,000 to 4,000 lines for 35mm

- 10,000 to 16,000 lines for 4"x5"
- 20,000 to 32,000 lines for 8"x10"

The following are estimates for file sizes for preservation quality scans of photographs—negatives or transparencies—based on the lower resolution limits cited above.

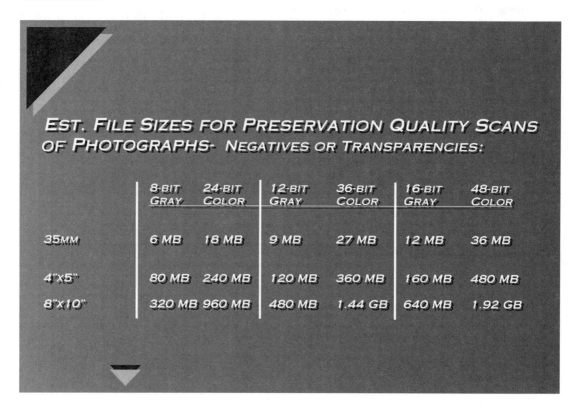

EST. FILE SIZES FOR PRESERVATION QUALITY SCANS OF PHOTOGRAPHS- NEGATIVES OR TRANSPARENCIES:

	8-BIT GRAY	24-BIT COLOR	12-BIT GRAY	36-BIT COLOR	16-BIT GRAY	48-BIT COLOR
35MM	6 MB	18 MB	9 MB	27 MB	12 MB	36 MB
4"x5"	80 MB	240 MB	120 MB	360 MB	160 MB	480 MB
8"x10"	320 MB	960 MB	480 MB	1.44 GB	640 MB	1.92 GB

1.d. General or Minimum Digitizing Requirements for Facilitating Reproduction and Access

Cornell recommends 600 ppi for 1-bit scanning or 400 ppi for 8-bit scanning of printed type to achieve preservation quality scanning. Other general recommendations for reproduction are:

Textual records
200 to 600 ppi for 1-bit
200 to 400 ppi for 8-bit grayscale
200 to 300 ppi for 24-bit color

Photographs
3000 to 5000 lines for 8-bit grayscale
3000 to 5000 lines for 24-bit color

Maps/Plans/Oversized
200 to 300 ppi for 8-bit grayscale
200 to 300 ppi for 24-bit color

As computers become faster and memory becomes cheaper, the recommendations for scanning resolution are likely to increase. Today, projects are selecting higher scanning resolution than older digitizing projects.

2. Pixel Bit Depth

Computers work on a binary system; each bit of data is either a 1 or a 0. Each pixel in a raster image is represented by a string of binary digits. The number of digits is known as the bit depth. A 1-bit pixel is represented by one binary digit, either a 1 or a 0. A 2-bit pixel is represented by two binary digits, either — 0 + 0, 0 + 1, 1 + 0, or 1 + 1. The bit depth determines the number of possible combinations of 1s and 0s for that number of binary digits and therefore the number of gray shades or color shades that can be represented by each pixel, as illustrated by the following formula.

Number of shades = 2^x X = the bit depth

1 bit = 2 shades (a single binary digit- a single 1 or a single 0 — (black or white)
2 bits = 4 shades (two binary digits form four possible combinations — black, dark gray, light gray, and white)
3 bits = 8 shades (three binary digits form 8 possible combinations)
4 bits = 16 shades (four binary digits form 16 possible combinations)
5 bits = 32 shades (five binary digits form 32 possible combinations)
6 bits = 64 shades (six binary digits form 64 possible combinations)
7 bits = 128 shades (seven binary digits form 128 possible combinations)
8 bits = 256 shades (eight binary digits form 256 possible combinations
10 bits = 1,024 shades (ten binary digits form 1,024 possible combinations)
12 bits = 4,096 shades (twelve binary digits form 4,096 possible combinations)
14 bits = 16,384 shades (fourteen binary digits form 16,384 possible combinations)
16 bits = 65,536 shades (sixteen binary digits form 65,536 possible combinations)

Bit Depth Illustrations

The following are current standard bit depths for image files.

1-bit	black-and-white
8-bit grayscale	256 shades of gray
8-bit color	256 colors
24-bit RGB*	approximately 17 million colors, three 8-bit channels

*See next section

The bit depth influences the representation of images. Obviously, at 1-bit there are only black or white values and no gray shading. Texture and other subtle shading values are not reproduced. At 2-bits, four shades are reproduced — black, white, and two intermediate shades of gray. At 4-bits, 16 shades are reproduced, and the background texture of a document will be rendered. At 6-bit grayscale, 64 shades of gray, the digital image approximates typical human perceptual response. Psychometric studies have determined that most people can distinguish approximately 64 shades of gray. Years ago, when computer scientists were establishing conventions for digital imaging, computer memory was expensive and CPU speed was slow. It was an easy decision to limit grayscale image files to 8-bits to save storage space, since the 256 shades reproduced exceeds human perception. However, 8-bit grayscales' rendering of 256 shades is limited compared to photographic materials and can present problems when the contrast and brightness of digital images needs to be adjusted. The use of 8-bit grayscale image files, and corresponding 24-bit RGB color image files (three color channels of 8-bit information), was a reasonable compromise and, in many cases, still is.

3. Color
Color Systems
Several different systems are used to represent color images. The most common are RGB (additive color system), CMYK (subtractive color system), and the CIE-L*A*B* color space, a mathematical modeling of color.

RGB The additive color system combines variations of red, green, and blue (RGB) to form white. This method is used in the design of televisions, computer monitors, and film recorders. Think of an RGB color image as three separate images superimposed one over the other. The superimposition is done mathematically. Basically, an RGB image consists of three 8-bit grayscale images or channels; one channel represents the red information, a second channel represents the green information, and the third channel represents the blue information. The computer mathematically combines the three channels for each pixel to determine the final color. A 24-bit RGB color digital image file consists of three channels each with 8-bits of data (3 channels x 8-bits = 24-bits).

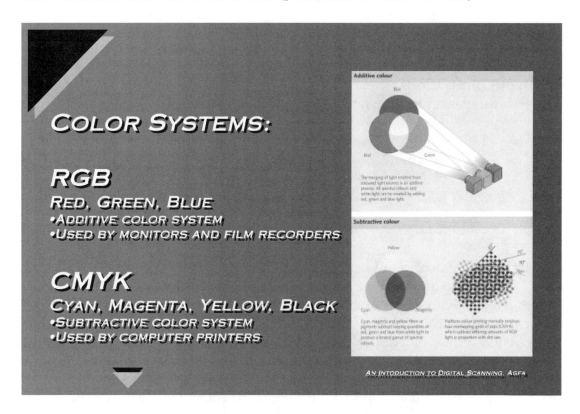

CMYK The subtractive color system combines variations of cyan, magenta, and yellow to form black. This method is used in the graphic arts printing process and with computer printers. Often, the printer uses a fourth ink, black, to increase the range of densities that can be reproduced. Four-color printers use cyan, magenta, yellow, and black (CMYK). Almost all color photographic materials have been based on subtractive color, utilizing varying amounts of cyan, magenta, and yellow dye. Most computer printers use four colors, although there are now printers on the market that have six colors; a light magenta and a light cyan have been added to improve the image quality when printing photographic images. A 32-bit CMYK color digital image file consists of four channels, each with 8-bits of data (4 channels x 8-bits = 32-bits).

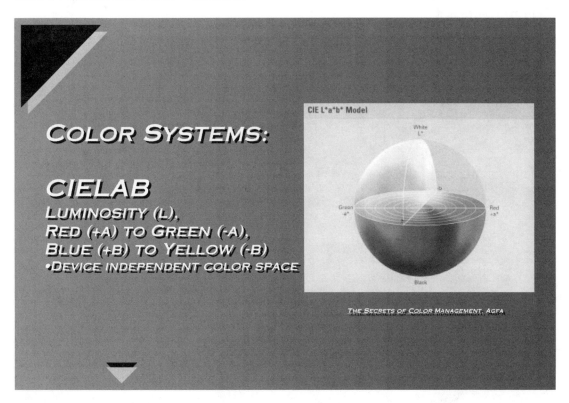

CIE-L*A*B* The CIE-L*A*B* color space is a mathematical model of color that divides the color into luminosity (L) that can be thought of as the grayscale information, red (+A) to green (-A) information, and blue (+B) to yellow (-B) information. The L*A*B* color space is referred to as a device-independent color space. It is not linked to a specific type of output device like a computer monitor (RGB) or a computer printer (CMYK). A 24-bit L*A*B* color digital image file consists of three channels, each with 8-bits (3 channels x 8-bits = 24-bits).

Recommendations

Most scanners utilize RGB scanning, although some do convert the images to CMYK or L*A*B* images. For most digital imaging projects, it is recommended to save color images as RGB files, not as CMYK files. The L*A*B* color space could be used, but fewer software applications are able to interpret and use the L*A*B* files at this time. Since it is always possible to convert RGB files for output, CMYK image files should only be used for printing.

> **F**or most projects, save color images as RGB files.

The overriding objective in preservation is to save the most information that is economically possible, using methods that can be reversed if required.

Increasingly, scanners and software are able to handle high-bit image files. This means rather than having 8-bits per color channel, the files may have 10-bits, 12-bits or 16-bits per color channel. An RGB color image that has 16-bits per channel is a 48-bit color image file (3 channels x 16-bits = 48-bits).

Comparison

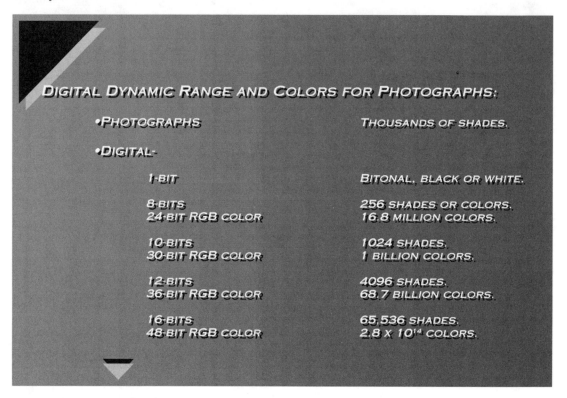

DIGITAL DYNAMIC RANGE AND COLORS FOR PHOTOGRAPHS:

• PHOTOGRAPHS	THOUSANDS OF SHADES.
• DIGITAL-	
1-BIT	BITONAL, BLACK OR WHITE.
8-BITS	256 SHADES OR COLORS.
24-BIT RGB COLOR	16.8 MILLION COLORS.
10-BITS	1024 SHADES.
30-BIT RGB COLOR	1 BILLION COLORS.
12-BITS	4096 SHADES.
36-BIT RGB COLOR	68.7 BILLION COLORS.
16-BITS	65,536 SHADES.
48-BIT RGB COLOR	2.8×10^{14} COLORS.

As can be seen from the chart, as the bit depth is increased, the number of shades and the number of colors that can be reproduced increases dramatically. Photographic materials are able to render effectively several thousand shades. The equivalent bit depth for digital imaging is at least 12-bits per channel.

Color Gamut

A color gamut is the range of colors that a system, such as a computer monitor or printer, can reproduce. Color gamuts are illustrated graphically to compare different color spaces, color systems, or devices. Wide gamut RGB and L*A*B* color spaces can render a greater range of colors and generally require the use of higher bit depths to achieve a wide color gamut. The CMYK color system has a limited color gamut and can reproduce a correspondingly limited range of colors; this is another reason not to use CMYK files for master image files.

Color Palettes

Color palettes are discrete sets of defined colors used by computers to represent 8-bit or 256-color images. The Windows and Macintosh operating systems use different sets of colors for 8-bit color images. The rendition of the image changes depending on which type of computer the image is viewed. One approach for 8-bit color file formats — such as GIF files intended to be distributed via the World Wide Web — is to use a Web-safe pallet. A Web-safe palette uses 212 to 216 common colors between the Windows and Macintosh palettes, and the image should look the same on either type of computer. Another option is an adaptive pallet, where the 256 colors used for the palette are based on the specific colors in a specific image. In most cases using an adaptive palette will make an 8-bit color image look much more like the original 24-bit color image, compared to using a Windows, Macintosh, or Web-safe palette.

Color Imbalance

Color imbalances happen when neutral values are not rendered with equal levels of red, green, and blue (obviously, for an RGB image file). As an example, a white highlight in a digital image will shift to a color when the tones are clipped in a single or two of the color channels.

Accuracy of Color

Managing the accuracy of color rendition for digital images is complex, involving the adjustment and calibration of computer monitors, the adjustment of scanner controls, the correction or enhancement of images using image processing software, the adjustment and calibration of output devices, and the use of color management software. This software transforms images between different color spaces to correct for differences in the color gamuts of scanners, monitors, and output devices. Apple's Colorsync and Windows ICM are examples of color management software that have been incorporated into the operating systems of computers.

Measuring Digital Values

Not all scanner or image processing controls work as well as expected, so it is often necessary to measure digital values — either RGB levels for color images or % black for grayscale images. Most image processing software applications have a control that allows a user to measure the digital values for a single pixel or a group of pixels in an image, such as the Eyedropper in Adobe Photoshop. It is important to set the options for the Eyedropper to the appropriate setting before measuring values. All digital images have noise (random pixels of the incorrect shade or color) that makes measuring individual pixels problematic. It is recommended to set the Eyedropper to the setting that averages a set of 5 x 5 pixels (a square of 25 pixels). This will average out the variation due to noise.

Digital Image Processing

Oversampling

As previously noted, digital images have bit depths of 1-bit per pixel for black and white images (common for document imaging), 8-bits per pixel grayscale for continuous tone images, and 24-bits per pixel for color images. Generally, scanners will sample at bit depths higher than these, and then the bit depth is reduced for the final image. This is known as oversampling. Scanners are designed to oversample to improve image quality by reducing noise (random pixels of the wrong shade), and extending the effective tonal scale of the scanner (initially measuring more shades than are used in the final image). This allows a larger density range to be represented without loss of detail — a problem when scanning color slides or transparencies and other very dense originals. Document scanners will sample at 8-bits to produce a 1-bit image, and a grayscale scanner will sample at 10-bits or 12-bits to produce an 8-bit image.

Image Processing Filters

Image processing filters — mathematical formulas that change the appearance of digital images — can be applied to improve the appearance of images and to assist with resizing images. Commonly, sharpening filters are used to enhance the appearance of digital image files. The need for sharpening is inversely proportional to the resolution of the digital image: lower resolution or smaller digital images tend to need more sharpening, and higher resolution or larger digital images tend to need less sharpening. Many people advocate not sharpening master image files, due to concern that the enhancement cannot be undone in the future. The most photographic sharpening filter is unsharp mask. This term comes from the graphic arts industry practice of using a reverse toned mask that is slightly out of focus to increase the visual sharpness of images. It is possible to over-sharpen an image: Over-sharpening with an unsharp mask filter will create light halos around sharp edges within images.

Another filter commonly used when resizing images is the blur filter. Slightly blurring an image creates additional shading along sharply defined edges in an image, which can allow the interpolation software do a better job when the image is resized. Most images have to be sharpened after resizing, whether or not a blur filter is applied.

Just as with interpolation algorithms, some image-processing filter algorithms will do a better job in terms of image quality than other algorithms, while others might work faster. Again, generally the filters in more expensive image processing software will tend to do a better job with image quality compared to the filters in less expensive software.

Histogram

A common image-processing tool is the histogram, found in most image processing software packages. The histogram is a graphic representation of the distribution of gray shades in an image. The height of each vertical line is proportional to the number of pixels that are of that shade — the taller the line the more pixels of that shade. Also, the histogram can give indications of certain types of image defects, such as loss of tones in the shadows (dark values or shades) or the highlights (light values or shades) of an image. The histogram illustrates and helps our understanding of the concept of thresholding.

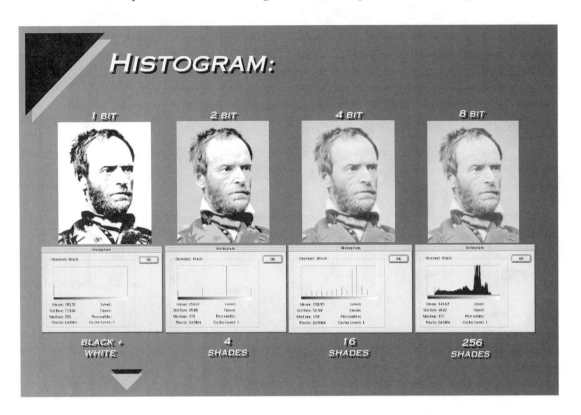

Thresholding

Thresholding is a technique used in image processing to convert gray shades to either black or white. All shades lower than a selected value are rendered as white and all shades higher are rendered as black. Depending on the value selected for the threshold, the representation of the same image can be altered dramatically. Most 1-bit scanners actually sample at 8 bits, but then a threshold value is used to convert the 8-bit image to a 1-bit image.

When are there problems using 1-bit digitization and thresholding? In cases of thermofax, verifax, or carbon copy processes where the paper ages as it darkens and the type fades, it is very difficult to reproduce the image with a 1-bit scan regardless of the threshold level. At lower threshold values the characters appear incomplete. As the threshold value is increased, the characters will quickly fill in (*e.g.,* the letter "o" becomes a very large dot) and only the context within the word or sentence provides an idea of the character. Further increasing the level of the threshold will cause pixels representing shading in the background to turn black, an effect that is known as speckle. There are software programs designed to work with 1-bit scanning designed to despeckle an image. The software tries to remove extraneous black pixels in the image. Unfortunately, this doesn't always work the way you want. Parameters for despeckling can be adjusted, based on the size of the speckle you want to remove, but as the size of the speckle to be removed is increased, it will start removing periods, dots of "i"s, and other necessary punctuation.

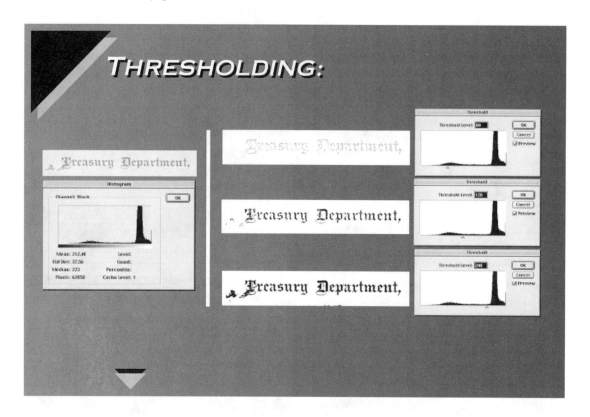

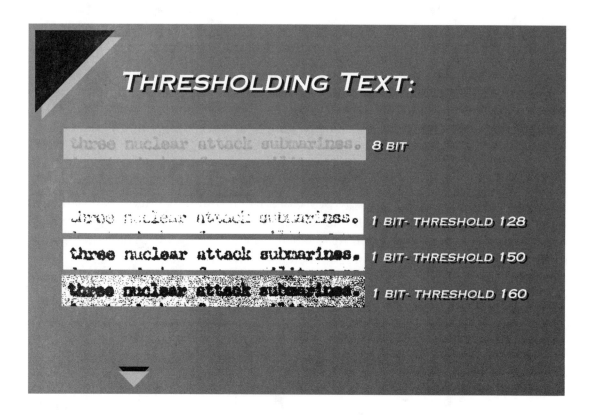

Dithering

When using low bit depth images, it is possible to simulate a greater number of shades with fewer shades. This process is known as dithering. The key is to redistribute pixels according to a mathematical formula to produce synthetic shades of gray based on the arrangement of these pixels and the way the eye perceives them. There are different formulas for dithering, and some work better than others. If an 8-bit grayscale image is converted to a 3-bit image without dithering, broad areas of similar shades will be rendered as a single shade. In photographic terms, this effect is known as posterization. In digital images, this effect is sometimes referred to as banding, particularly when it appears across broad shade gradients, such as skies in photographs. When a 24-bit color image is converted to an 8-bit color image, the 8-bit file can be dithered. Dithering and an adaptive grayscale palette can be used to provide a very accurate rendition of an image with bit depths as low as 4-bits or 16 shades.

Tonal Controls

Each image processing software application has different controls for adjusting the tones and color balance of digital images. In Adobe PhotoShop, one of the most common image processing software packages, the preferred controls for tonal adjustments and color correction are *Levels and Curves*. Other controls are available in PhotoShop, such as *Contrast and Brightness* and *Color Balance*, but they are global corrections that influence all tones of the image. *Levels and Curves* offers greater control with less risk of losing information while adjusting images.

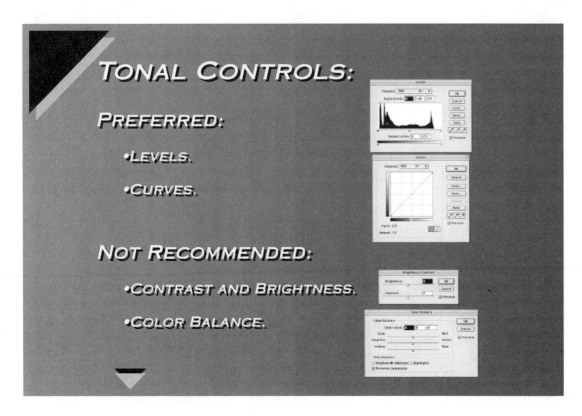

Tonal Scale Comparisons

The bit depth of a digital image has a big influence on how accurately an original document, photograph, or book is rendered in terms of the tones of the original. The tone reproduction for a 1-bit digital image is somewhat similar to the tonal response of microfilm — high contrast and most suitable for rendering clean, printed type. An 8-bit grayscale image is more similar to continuous tone black-and-white photographic films used in still photography — lower contrast and able to render a greater range of tones.

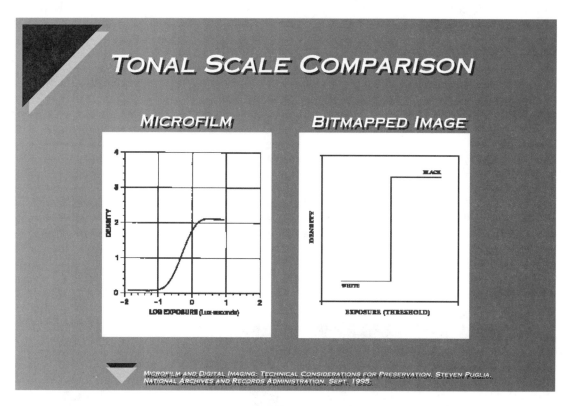

One way to compare tonal responses is to look at the characteristic curves for photographic films and a similar graph for the digitization response. A characteristic curve is a graphic representation of the response of a film to both exposure and development. The horizontal axis is exposure; as you move to the right on the x-axis, exposure increases. The vertical axis is density. A typical characteristic curve for microfilm shows that as exposure increases, there is a proportional large increase in density. The rate of increase in density compared to exposure, which is the slope of the line, is the contrast. Microfilm is a high-contrast photographic film with a limited range of tones that can be distinguished. This is somewhat similar to 1-bit (bitonal) digital images. In bitonal images, all tonal values on the original that are lighter than a selected tone will be rendered white, and all tonal values darker than the selected tone will be rendered black. The point at which the tones shift from white to black is the threshold value. Anything lighter than the threshold value will be rendered white, everything darker than the threshold value will be rendered black. The 1-bit digitization response is similar to microfilm. However, despite being high contrast, microfilm

Handbook For Digital Projects

does have a range of shades unlike 1-bit images, which only have black or white values (all gray shades are eliminated).

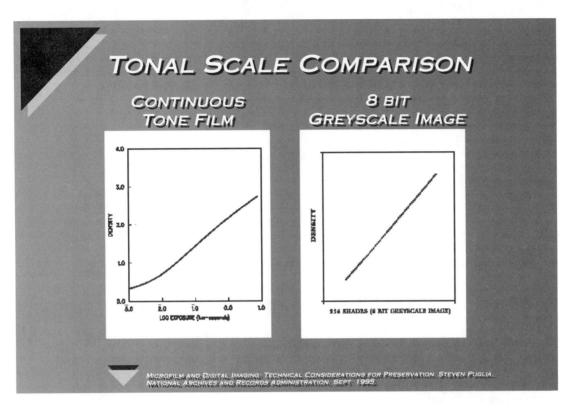

If you look at the characteristic curve of a continuous-tone black-and-white still photography film, the curve looks different because the contrast is lower and, for most of these films, the length of the characteristic curve is longer. Both of these properties mean that a still photography film can render more shades, equivalent to scanning at a higher bit depth, and correspondingly can distinguish more shades. An 8-bit gray scale image has a response that is relatively similar to continuous-tone photographic films. However, an 8-bit image has a maximum of only 256 shades or levels. Most photographic films can effectively distinguish thousands of shades.

Clipping

Clipping happens when image detail is rendered as white or black and the image detail is lost. Once the tones have been clipped, it is not possible to get the tones back. It is important to adjust scanner controls to minimize clipping during scanning. Then, it is important to avoid clipping when using the tonal and color adjustment controls of image processing software.

Digital Image File Structure

The digital data that represent a complete image are contained within a computer file. The string of binary digits is arranged into an organized structure that allows the computer and software to interpret the data and recreate the image. A digital image file has several major parts.

Simple image file structure (from *"Structures and Metrics for Image Storage and Interchange,"* JEI, Journal of Electronic Imaging *co-published by SPIE [the International Society of Optical Engineering] and IS&T [the Society for Imaging Science and Technology],* April 1993).

Header
- A file identifier
- Image specification

Image Data
- Look-up table
- Image raster

Footer
- File terminator

The file header identifies a digital file for the computer and includes an image specification indicating the file format. The image data section of the file, which in some cases includes a look-up table, follows the header. The look-up table is a defined set of colors or shades of gray that tells the computer how to represent the image on a computer monitor. The image raster is the strings of 1s and 0s representing each of the individual pixels representing a bitmap image. The final part of the file, the footer, tells the computer the entire file has been opened or downloaded.

Data and File Compression

Data and file compression is the process of reducing, through various means, the amount of data to be stored or transmitted. There are two broad categories of compression: **lossless** allows file reconstruction that is identical to the original and **lossy** discards certain amount of original information during the compression process. Some of the compression algorithms include:

LZW (Lempel-Ziv-Welch) — lossless
JPEG (Joint Photographic Experts Group) — lossy
MPEG (Moving Pictures Experts Group) — lossy
Wavelet — lossy
Fractal — lossy

Reformatting Comparison

Original documents with clean, printed type or text (with high inherent contrast between the type/text and the background, and sharply defined characters) can be reproduced using 1-bit scanning in the digital environment. This is comparable to traditional microfilm. If documents have low inherent contrast between the type/text, if characters have diffuse edges (such as carbon copies or other types of copy processes), or if there are photographs, then you should digitize with 8-bits (256 shades of gray) at a minimum, or use a low- to medium-contrast,

REFORMATTING COMPARISON:

ORIGINAL DOCUMENT	DIGITAL IMAGING	PHOTOGRAPHIC
PRINTED TEXT (GOOD CONDITION)	1 BIT / BITONAL BLACK AND WHITE	MICROFILM / HIGH CONTRAST
LOW CONTRAST TEXT AND PHOTOGRAPHS	8 BIT / 256 LEVEL GREYSCALE	CONT. TONE FILM / LOW TO MED. CONTRAST
COLOR GRAPHICS / TEXT AND COLOR PHOTOS	24 BIT (RGB) / 16 MIL. COLORS	COLOR FILM / LOW TO MED. CONTRAST

MICROFILM AND DIGITAL IMAGING: TECHNICAL CONSIDERATIONS FOR PRESERVATION. STEVEN PUGLIA, NATIONAL ARCHIVES AND RECORDS ADMINISTRATION. SEPT. 1995.

continuous-tone photographic film. Finally, for color graphics, color text, or color photographs, you need to capture the color information in addition to shading. At a minimum, digitization should be done as 24-bit RGB (16 million colors) scanning; you can also use color photographic color.

———

Contributing to this chapter was Don Willis, whose earlier role in preservation is cited in Chapter VII: Case Studies—Working with Microfilm.

Sources

Besser, Howard and Jennifer Trant. *Introduction to Imaging: Issues in Constructing an Image Database*. Getty Art History Information Program, Santa Monica, CA, 1995. [Online] http://www.getty.edu/gri/standard/introimages/

Frey, Franziska and James Reilly. *Digital Imaging for Photographic Collections: Foundations for Technical Standards*. Image Permanence Institute, Rochester Institute of Technology, Rochester, NY, 1999. [Online] http://www.rit.edu/~661www1/sub_pages/frameset2.html

A Guide to Digital Photography: Theory and Basics. Agfa Educational Publishing, Randolph, MA. [Online] http://www.agfahome.com/publications/

An Introduction to Digital Scanning. Agfa Educational Publishing, Randolph, MA. [Online] http://www.agfahome.com/publications/

Kenney, Anne and Oya Rieger. *Moving Theory Into Practice: Digital Imaging for Libraries and Archives*. Research Libraries Group, Mountain View, CA, 2000. [Online] http://www.rlg.org/preserv/mtip-order.html

Kodak Digital Learning Center. [Online] http://www.kodak.com/US/en/digital/dlc/book3/

RLG DigiNews on-line newsletter. [Online] http://www.rlg.org/preserv/diginews/

The Secrets of Color Management. Agfa Educational Publishing, Randolph, MA. [Online] http://www.agfahome.com/publications/

VII
Developing Best Practices: Guidelines from Case Studies

Introduction

This chapter contains six case studies that move the reader from the theoretical views of how digitization should be conducted to the actual practice of planning, executing, and evaluating projects. Some of the sections focus primarily on the experiences of one institution, while other sections are composites of what has been learned from various situations.

The case studies include descriptions of what has worked and has not worked. Wherever possible, authors have included tips for those who are beginning new scanning projects.

1. Working with Printed Text and Manuscripts

Stephen Chapman
Harvard University Library

Look at the growing body of network-accessible books, journals, and archives from cultural institutions and commercial publishers and you will discover that electronic text is not all alike. Some collections are searchable, others are not; some have high-quality color reproductions, others limit their content to black-and-white (1-bit) images; some support go-to-page and go-to-section navigation, and many simply provide page-forward, page-back functionality. Rather than present a single case study of one type of electronic text, this section presents a composite case study of the challenges raised by several types of text conversion and the guidelines that have emerged in response to them.

Since costs among all of these versions vary widely, the first job for the budget-conscious manager is to select the least-expensive electronic publication model appropriate to the collection(s) she or he has selected for digitization. Generally speaking, electronic text falls into three categories:

> *Page Images* These *digital photocopies* are created by scanning printed pages or microfilm. Page images are not searchable. They may be black-and-white, grayscale, or color. Assume that black-and-white (1-bit) page images are the least expensive products of text digitization, but be sure to account for the associated costs of the structural metadata that is needed in order to make the images suitable for browsing and on-line navigation.

> *Full Text* In order for printed text to become fully searchable electronic text (full text), the letters on the original pages must be translated to machine-processible ASCII. There are two ways to do this: either by typing from the original (known as *keying*) or by using an optical character recognition (OCR) program to convert page images to ASCII. The first process is manual, the second automated. Since keying can easily be ten times more expensive than scanning-plus-OCR, page images are often made to facilitate the creation of full text. When these two products (full text and page images) are made, there is the added advantage of being able to present a *facsimile* version of the original page — with fonts, formatting, marginalia, and illustrations intact — in response to a search. In other words, the ASCII is used to create an index for searching, and only the page images are delivered to the screen or printer.

One might ask: If scanning and OCR are so much cheaper than keying, why consider keying at all? First, OCR is viable only for page images of machine-printed text. Handwritten originals must be keyed to become searchable. Second, OCR accuracy decreases as the complexity of originals increases (number of fonts, number of columns, illustrations accompanying text), and as the quality of the page images decreases. Therefore, if near 100% accuracy of searching is required, it might be less expensive to key than to undertake the three-step process of scan, OCR, and correct OCR errors. Several reliable studies report that a trained technician can correct 6-10 pages per hour. Depending upon salary, this task alone could easily exceed the cost of keying.

Encoded Text, or Full Text with Mark-up This third publishing model for text conversion is the most expensive, but also the most functional and flexible in the online environment. Like plain full text, encoded text production requires keying or OCR of page images to create ASCII. The final step is to encode attributes of a given document by placing Standard Generalized Markup Language (SGML) tags around selected text. There are hundreds of SGML elements that can be used for encoding. The Text Encoding Initiative (TEI) Guidelines refer to a subset that has been used widely for publications in the humanities. Texts usually are encoded at one or both of the following levels: (1) structural: referring to divisions such as chapters within books, articles within journals, poems within anthologies; or (2) descriptive: referring to elements such as dates, names of persons or places, and occupations. When a properly configured search interface/application is coupled with an SGML database, encoding makes fielded searching possible (*e.g.,* find "slavery" in captions), and can also be used to control the presentation of the document — including multiple representations if desired.

Note: It is not necessary to create page images in order to produce encoded text if (1) keying is an affordable approach to production, and (2) your goal is to present modern rather than facsimile pages to the screen or printer.

After deciding which electronic products satisfy the project requirements, the manager's second task should be to specify the outcome for the source materials after conversion. Since the printed originals are also products of text conversion, it is important to determine whether they should emerge exactly as they began or whether alterations are acceptable. It is significantly easier to create a project budget and plan of work if disposition decisions — related to access policies, materials housing and location, and even deaccessioning — are made at the outset.

Decisions about the appropriate outcomes for the source materials inform, if not determine, the handling guidelines for scanning. Materials that will be kept, particularly if they are to remain as circulating copies, may need to be assessed, cleaned, repaired, or rehoused at some point in the project. On the other hand, materials that will be moved to offsite storage or even discarded allow for a greater range of options in scanning techniques.

Questions about handling and disposition are particularly important for bound materials. Disbound pages, even when highly brittle, can either be scanned on flatbed scanners or can be automatically fed to sheetfeed scanners (with straight paper paths). In other words, it is much less expensive to scan pages than to scan books. As of 1999, production statistics gathered from a number of projects indicate that although technicians can scan up to five pages per minute, they typically average between two and three. Auto-feed scanners, on the other hand, can scan two sides of a page in a single pass. Using the same output settings (*e.g.,* 600 dpi 1-bit TIFF), these scanners produce 20 images per minute. Thus, assessments of source materials are critical because whenever manual feeding (or page turning) is required, scanning prices are tied directly to labor costs. In this model, improvements in scanning technology can only result in better quality, but not higher speed. When auto-feeding is allowed, technology improvements can result not only in higher quality but also higher speeds, and therefore lower unit costs.

Decisions regarding appropriate handling are complex, and any method must be tested and confirmed with a sample of materials before undertaking full production. No single best system has emerged for text scanning. Auto-feed, flatbed, overhead, or even digital camera systems are all viable. When selecting a scanner or writing specifications for a service bureau, handling requirements should be specified first, then image quality and speed. Scanning software plays an important role in these areas. For example, the same input settings — *e.g.,* 600 dpi 1-bit TIFF — on different scanners will produce different results on output. Batch settings often distinguish high-price from low-price systems and are critical for high-volume applications.

Rules of Thumb

Although there are many variables associated with selecting the best methods to create page images and/or full text, there are fortunately some rules of thumb common to many text conversion projects.

- To minimize costs of creating and maintaining page images, 1-bit scanning with lossless compression should be used whenever possible; permitting the use of auto-feed scanners is the least expensive way to produce images of high enough quality for OCR, printing, and/or computer output microfilm (COM). Quality from all 1-bit scanners — sheetfeed, flatbed, and overhead — is the product of engineering (hardware, optics), software, and operator skill, so be sure to confirm that resolution requirements cited in one project work equally well for the materials and scanner you have selected in yours.
- When grayscale or color scanning is preferred for machine-printed text, use a scanner or digital camera with enough spatial resolution to capture the lines, edges, and other details of the source materials. Compare the costs and quality of line-array and area-array systems to determine which produces acceptable

quality at the lowest cost. If OCR is required, fairly sophisticated image processing (following scanning) will be needed to generate 1-bit files from the grayscale or color scans.

- When conservation assessment and/or treatment is mandated for the source materials, conservators should participate in selecting the scanning equipment that will be used and in writing the handling guidelines for the project.

- Image quality and quality control requirements relate directly to the disposition of the source materials. Quality requirements will be higher for projects where reduced access to, or even replacement of, the originals is required. Costs, ironically, may be lower, since auto-feeding may be viewed as a more acceptable technique for these items than for unique materials in good condition.

- Costs of document preparation (excluding conservation treatment), metadata creation, and quality control are likely to exceed the cost of scanning, particularly for 1-bit imaging.

- Given the design of overhead scanners, as well as the limited depth of field in many digital cameras, bound volumes will be less expensive to scan if they can be opened fully (180 degrees). Text printed near or into the gutter margin is always difficult to capture — as handling requirements increase, so will the costs.

- Oversize pages (particularly when the longest dimension is greater than 17") are always more expensive to scan. High-quality digital reproduction of text becomes more difficult with direct scanning; newspapers, for example, have routinely been microfilmed first in order to produce page images of adequate quality.

- Many image enhancement techniques, such as despeckling and deskewing, can be automated following scanning. Image processing is important not only to the appearance of page images, but also to their optimization for OCR.

- The structural metadata needed to organize page images may be created before, during, or after scanning. Given the idiosyncrasies of pagination and organization of many historic collections, one should expect these tasks to be manual, or semiautomated at best.

- Requirements for full text accuracy and depth of encoding result from a careful analysis of the source materials and consultation with the community(ies) interested in using the digital collections.

The following table summarizes the decisions that have the most important impact on quality and cost in text conversion projects. Many guidelines have been proposed from case studies, and these have been generalized for the table. As discussed in other chapters, however, good management begins by setting goals, not by blindly following guidelines. Relate your decisions to your publication objectives and preferred outcomes for the source materials, and the scanning guidelines and costs will naturally follow.

KEY QUALITY AND COST DECISIONS FOR DIGITIZED TEXT

Product	Examples of Key Decisions	Guidelines
Source Materials	*Handling* ■ Contact with glass permitted	All scanners are viable
	■ Bound volumes must be supported during scanning (opened less than 180°)	Face-up scanning required, with appropriate cradle/book support
	Disposition ■ Maintain standard of access: return in original format to original location	Identify resources available for treatment. If staffing and funding are available, for example, to assess, disbind, and rebind materials, then compare costs of scanning pages versus scanning books before selecting best approach.
	■ Reduce access by changing circulation policy or by relocating	To save cost, auto-feed if feasible, but budget for necessary preparation material and rehousing costs.
	■ Severely reduce or even eliminate access by creating digital images of replacement quality and/or by disposing source materials after scanning	Requirements for quality control and metadata must be explicitly defined (consider use of technical targets); disbinding might be most appropriate in these circumstances.
	Preparation ■ Facilitate highest quality scanning at the lowest cost	Segregate materials into batches whenever feasible (*e.g.*, by size; or by content — text, illustration, mixed, color)
Page Images	*Specifications for master (archival) images* ■ Achieve tone reproduction appropriate to source materials and output requirements	When black-and-white (1-bit) fails to capture essential information, use scanners that sample 12-bits per pixel and output at least 8-bits per pixel for grayscale and 24-bits per pixel for color.
	■ For machine-printed text, achieve detail reproduction needed to meet output requirements (screen, print, OCR for machine-printed text)	400-600 dpi commonly used; threshold and image processing capabilities also critical to image quality, especially for 1-bit images; post-scan enhancements can increase OCR accuracy
	■ For handwritten manuscripts and soft-edge type, such as photostats, achieve detail reproduction needed to meet output requirements (screen, print, zoom)	300 dpi minimum for 1-bit, 200-400 dpi minimum for grayscale and color

Product	Examples of Key Decisions	Guidelines
	■ Use open format	TIFF
	■ Use safe compression	Group 4 (lossless) compression for 1-bit, none for grayscale and color images
	■ Implement quality control program	Confirm that all files for object have been received, sequence is correct, metadata is complete and correct (100%); check image quality on screen, in print or both (sample)
	Specifications for delivery images (derivatives) ■ Print, computer-output microfilm (COM)	Master images (high-resolution TIFFs), PDF, or Postscript
	■ On-screen images	Legibility generally achieved at 80-120 dpi; minimize file size by using fewer than the full 8-bits for GIF whenever possible (*e.g.,* 4-bit); if 8 to 24-bits are required, consider JPEG
	Specifications for navigation ■ Page-forward, page back	Include *sequence* field in image database, or embed sequence in filenames
	■ Go-to page	Include *page number* field in image database, or embed page number in filenames (the latter is generally a more expensive solution)
	■ Go-to section	Include *feature* or *feature code* field in image database, or mark-up full text (see below)
Full Text	*Specification for accuracy (characters only)* ■ 100%	Get prices for keying first, then conduct sample OCR test of page images
	■ less than 100%	Conduct sample OCR test of page images and review acceptability of output; avoid need to correct OCR-generated text at all costs

Product	Examples of Key Decisions	Guidelines
Marked-up Text	*Specification for accuracy (characters and formatting)* ■ Fidelity to original required desirable	Keying/encoding may be the least expensive approach; test scanning/ OCR only if the original layout and fonts are relatively simple
	Specification for encoding ■ Accommodate attributes of materials in hand while using practices endorsed by broader community	Consult TEI LITE and create DTD to accommodate structural divisions and descriptive features in the texts in hand; local interpretations of the general guidelines are possible

Sources

Bicknese, Douglas A. *Measuring the Accuracy of the OCR in the Making of America.* Winter1998. http://moa.umdl.umich.edu/moaocr.html

Guthrie, Kevin M. "JSTOR: From Project to Independent Organization." *D-Lib Magazine* (July-August, 1997). http://www.dlib.org/dlib/july97/07guthrie.html

Morrison, Alan, Michael Popham and Karen Wikander. "Creating and Documenting Electronic Texts: A Guide to Good Practice." *AHDS Guides to Good Practice.* Arts and Humanities Data Service, 2000. http://ota.ahds.ac.uk/documents/creating/

Text Endocding Initiative (TEI). "The TEI Consortium Homepage." http://www.ctei-c.org/

University of Virginia Library Electronic Text Center. The Electronic Text Center: On-Line Helpsheets. http://etext.lib.virginia.edu/helpsheets/sgmlscan.html

2. Working with Photographs

Franziska Frey
Image Permanence Institute

Why are Photographs Different?

There are several issues that set photographs apart from other documents for scanning.

Permanence

The materials that make up photographs are not chemically stable. These materials include silver or dyes as image-forming materials; paper, celluloid, or other plastics as base materials; and gelatin, albumen, or collodion as binders. Environmental influences such as light, chemical agents, heat, humidity, and storage conditions affect and destroy photographic materials. The only reliable method to preserve them for a long period of time is dark storage at low temperature and low humidity.

Faced with deterioration in the form of color dye fading, vinegar syndrome in acetate film, and degrading and flammable nitrate film, collection managers are debating whether it is better to invest in improved storage or in reformatting.

Complexity

Many digitization projects for photographs grew out of projects primarily dealing with text. This approach can lead to problems because images have to be treated quite differently when digitized.

The main goal when digitizing text documents is legibility. However, there are many different aspects of quality to be considered when digitizing images. In addition, finding aids for images are quite complex. Research is still underway to determine how best to facilitate effective searches.

Survey of Collection

Before a digitization project starts, the collection should be carefully surveyed. Not only the images but also the cataloguing system should be evaluated. In the long run, the inadequacy of the current image-description methods and the enormous amount of cataloging yet to be done with image collections will be the factors that restrict progress toward a digital future, rather than the lack of suitable imaging technology.

> Cataloging yet to be done will restrict progress, rather than the lack of technology.

Types of Photographs

Photographs can be classified into two groups according to whether the image is viewed by reflected or transmitted light. The most important difference between the two is in dynamic range — the difference between the lightest and the darkest areas of the image. Reflection prints of any type usually have a smaller dynamic range than negatives. Color transparencies have the largest dynamic range.

Negatives Negative collections especially profit from digitization since this makes them easily accessible. Millions of negatives are never used only because their image content is not readily available to the user. A printing process is needed to get a positive image. Therefore, not only the public but also often even the collection managers themselves don't know what a negative collection contains. It has already been proven that as soon as negatives are scanned and a positive image can be viewed, almost instantaneously their use has grown enormously. A huge number of older negatives are glass plate negatives. Choosing to digitize them reduces the risk of loss through breakage because they only have to be handled once.

Color Type Another way to classify images is by color type. Depending on the color type, images will be scanned in black-and-white or color.

Full Color— Most of today's photographs are taken in full color. However, this trend only dates back to the mid-1960's. This means that the majority of collections will not include too many color photographs, a fact that will change when more color photographs come into archives and libraries.

Monochromatic Color — A large number of photographs to be scanned will be monochromatic color (Reilly). Many 19th-century photographic print processes have characteristic colors, *e.g.*, the purplish-brown colors of albumen prints and the blue color of cyanotypes. Such colors help scholarly interpretation by conveying information about process and providing clues to the degree of deterioration the photographs may have suffered. Keeping this color information in the digital file is important since it is an inherent characteristic of the picture.

Black and White — Black and white photographs taken in monochrome are either neutral black in color or have no significant visual information conveyed by the color of the images. Primarily, these are negatives or modern silver-gelatin developed-out prints made in the 20th century.

Electronic Photography More and more, collections include images that never had a film original. Caring for electronic originals requires collection managers to pay attention to new specialties such as file formats, intellectual property law, high-speed data transfer technology, and database management.

Formats

Image collections often will have a variety of formats, although certain formats (*e.g.,* negatives, prints) can predominate. This variety requires the use of versatile scanning equipment.

Condition of Collection

A collection survey prior to scanning will help with decisions about what should be selected. It also can lead to a plan to control conditions of the original collection in the future, for example by providing better storage facilities or enclosure materials. Preparing a collection for scanning often includes an improvement of the physical conditions of the collection.

Size of Collection

The size of the collection also influences the scanning method and parameters. If the collection is very small, you can choose a time-consuming scanning method. A good example is the National Gallery in London, which scanned every painting using a special multispectral camera. Since the collection consists of only 3,000 paintings, it was possible to scan everything several times. This is not a possible solution for a collection that consists of thousands of images that will most likely not be rescanned within the near future. In addition, with larger collections the workflow has to be planned carefully.

Goals of Digitization

As the digitization of large collections is not likely to be attempted more than once a generation due to cost, educated decisions about the scanning and archiving processes are imperative. The term *archival* implies that all digitized images are not only optimized for current work flows and imaging devices but will continue to be usable on future, as yet unknown delivery and output systems (Frey & Süsstrunk, 1996; Frey, 1997; Frey & Süsstrunk, 1997).

One of the big issues that institutions should consider prior to implementing a project is the anticipated use of their digital image collections. There is a consensus within the preservation community that a number of image files must be created from every photograph to meet a range of uses. First, an archive or master image should be created. The archival master file should represent the highest quality the institution can afford. It should not be treated for any specific output and should be left uncompressed or compressed in a lossless manner. It will also require an intensive quality review. From this archive file, various derivatives will be calculated. These derivative files are meant to be used. Speed of access and transmission and suitability for certain purposes are the main issues to consider in the creation of these derivative files.

Scan from Duplicate or Original?

A decision has to be made whether to scan from the original or a duplicate. There are advantages and disadvantages to each approach. Because every generation of photographic copying involves some quality loss, using intermediates immediately implies some decrease in quality. Intermediates may also serve some other purposes, however; for example, they might serve as masters for photographic references copies or as preservation surrogates.

This leads to the question of whether the negative or the print should be used for digitization, assuming both are available. Quality will always be best if the first generation of an image (*i.e.,* the negative), is used. However, there may be big differences between the negative and the print, mainly in the domain of fine-art photography. The artist often spends a lot of time in the darkroom creating the print. The results of all this work are lost if the negative, rather than the print, is scanned. The outcome of the digitization will be disappointing.

Quality Control

Subjective Visual Inspection

The best approach to digital image quality control includes, on the one hand, subjective visual inspection and, on the other hand, objective measurements performed in software and on the digital files themselves. Efforts should be made to standardize the procedures and equipment for subjective evaluation.

In most cases the first evaluation of a scanned image will be made by viewing it on a monitor. The viewer will decide whether the image on the monitor fulfills the goals that have been stated at the beginning of the scanning project. This is important because human judgment decides the final acceptability of an image. Looking at images and judging their quality has always been a complex task. The viewer has to know what he/she is looking for. It should be emphasized that subjective quality control must be executed on calibrated equipment in an appropriate, standardized viewing environment

As the image is viewed on the monitor, defects such as dirt, half images, skew, laterally reversed images, and visual sharpness can be detected. In some cases it might be necessary to go back and redo the scanning.

Evaluating Digital Image Files

On the other hand, objective image quality parameters must be employed. You can accomplish this by scanning special targets and evaluating them in specialized software (Gann, 1999; Holm, "Survey," 1996).

The targets and software to evaluate them are not just for vendor checking — they serve to guarantee the long-term usefulness of the digital files and to protect the investments of the institutions.

Image Quality Framework

When looking at image quality, the whole image processing chain has to be examined (Holm, "Factors," 1996). Besides the scanning system, you also need to look at compression, file formats, image processing for various usage, and system calibration. Image quality is affected by the sequence of applying different image processing steps, including compression. Image processing done before storing the images can affect the quality of future processing. For example, it is recommended not to sharpen the archival master file before storing.

Each of the main image quality parameters needs special targets for the different forms of images (*e.g.,* prints, transparencies). The targets should consist of the same material as the materials that will be scanned — photographic film and paper.

These targets are a vital part of the image quality framework. After targets are scanned they are evaluated with a software program. Some software components exist as plug-ins to full-featured image browsers, others as stand-alone programs. However, it has to be clearly stated that some of the targets and the software to evaluate them are not yet commercially available.

Targets can be incorporated into the workflow in various ways. Full versions of the targets might be scanned every few hundred images and then linked to specific batches of production files, or smaller versions of the targets might be included with every image. As more institutions initiate digitization projects, having an objective tool to compare different scanning devices will be more and more important.

Tone Reproduction

Tone reproduction is the single most important parameter for determining the quality of an image. If the tone reproduction on an image is right, users will generally find the image acceptable, even is some of the other parameters are not optimal. Capture and display must occur for the concept of tone reproduction to exist. This means that an assumption must be made regarding the final viewing device. Three mutually dependent attributes affect tone reproduction: the opto-electronic conversion function (OECF), dynamic range, and flare. The OECF shows the relationship between the optical densities of an original and the corresponding digital values of the file. Dynamic range refers to the capacity of the scanner to capture extreme density variations. The dynamic range of the scanner should meet or exceed the dynamic range of the original. Flare is generated by stray light in an optical system. Flare reduces the dynamic range of a scanner.

Color Reproduction

Several color reproduction intents can apply to a digital image. Perceptual intent, relative colorimetric intent, and absolute colorimetric intent are the terms often associated with the International Color Consortium (ICC). Perceptual intent is to create a pleasing image on a given medium under given viewing conditions. Relative colorimetric intent is to match, as closely as possible, the colors of the reproduction to the colors of the original, taking into account output media and viewing conditions. Absolute colorimetric intent is to reproduce colors as exactly as possible, independent of output media and viewing conditions.

Most of the available solutions for measuring and controlling color reproduction are geared towards the pre-press industry. However, when an image is scanned for archival purposes, the future use of the image is not yet known. Operator judgments regarding color and contrast cannot be reversed in a 24-bit RGB color system. Any output mapping different from the archived image's color space and gamma must be considered. Nevertheless, saving raw scanner data can create problems if the scanner characteristics are not well known and profiled.

One of the decisions is which color space to use. A color space is a geometric representation of colors in space, usually of three dimensions. The reason for the three dimensions is the human visual system that has three independent receptors and is therefore a three dimensional system. The most important attribute of a color space in an archival environment is that it be well defined. Furthermore, keep in mind that there is more than one solution to the problem. The right color space depends on the purpose and the use of the digital images (Süsstrunk, Buckley & Sven, 1999).

Resolution

A review of past digital projects has shown that people are most concerned about spatial resolution. This is not surprising, because of all the weak links in digital capture, spatial resolution has been the best understood by most people. Technology has evolved, however, and today reasonable spatial resolution is neither extremely expensive nor does it cost a lot to store large data files. Spatial resolution is the parameter to define detail and edge reproduction in an image. Details can be, for example, single hairs in a portrait. A good edge reproduction is critical for the visual sharpness of an image. Spatial resolution of a digital image, *i.e.,* the number of details an image contains, is usually defined by the number of pixels per inch (ppi). The higher the number of pixels per inch, the more fine details can be transferred from the original image to the digital file.

To find the equivalent number of pixels that describe the information content of a specific photographic emulsion is not a straightforward process. Format of the original, film grain, film resolution, exposure, and processing techniques have to be taken into consideration to accurately determine the actual information content of a specific picture.

The best measure of detail and resolution is the Modulation Transfer Function (MTF). The MTF is a graphical representation of image quality that eliminates the need for decision making by the observer.

Noise

Noise refers to random signal variations associated with detection and reproduction systems. In conventional photography, noise in an image is the graininess that can be perceived. It can be seen most easily in uniform density areas. Noise is an important attribute of electronic imaging systems. Standardization will assist users and manufacturers in determining the quality of images being produced by these systems. Test results for noise are twofold. First the noise level of the system can be determined, indicating how many bit levels of the image data are actually useful. Second, for image quality considerations, the signal-to-noise (S/N) ratio is the important factor to know. S/N evaluations show the effect of random noise on scan quality. Random noise, rather than bit-depth, is the primary limiting factor of the tonal resolution of the scanner. The test can consist in scanning a grayscale target twice. The two scans are subtracted and the standard deviation of the result is examined. The subtraction should remove all non-noise components (this is the image information) and the standard deviation is a good measure of random noise (Gann, 1999).

Costs

Budget Items

There are a variety of costs to consider (Puglia, 1999):

- Selection
- Preparation
- Cataloging/Description/Indexing
- Preservation/Conservation
- Production of Intermediates
- Digitization
- Quality Control of Images and Metadata
- Network Infrastructure
- Ongoing Costs of Maintenance of Images and Data

Initial Costs

Digital conversion accounts for approximately one-third of the initial costs. Other costs, primarily those connected to cataloging, administration and quality control, account for the remaining two-thirds.

Ongoing Costs

Often, project planning and budgeting stops after the creation of the digital assets. However, an important part of the budget involves the costs for refreshing and migration and for the support of systems. This all can be put together under the umbrella of *digital asset management*. It is difficult at this point in time to come up with exact numbers for this process. However, since both the archival community and the graphic industry are taking this approach, more and more real numbers will be available soon. Currently, it is estimated that 5% to 10% of the initial costs per image must be budgeted on a yearly basis to maintain the images into the future, even though migration and file conversion are not done on a yearly basis.

In-house vs. Outsourcing

Many pilot projects with image collections have been used to build up an in-house scanning facility. Although this is feasible for a small project, in a many cases it will be better and necessary to establish a good relationship with a vendor and outsource the whole imaging process. Even this approach requires a good knowledge of the imaging process, because all the parameters for imaging and building the system will have to be established by the institutions themselves. As the chapter on vendor relations emphasizes, it is very important to establish a good relationship with the vendor.

Conclusions

Many of the problems arising from the need to scan for an unknown future use are not yet solved, and there is a great deal of uncertainty about how to proceed. Those responsible for some of the large digital reformatting projects report the same problem: Rapid changes in technology make it difficult to choose the best time to set up a reformatting policy that will not be outdated tomorrow.

If institutions fail to communicate their needs, they won't obtain tools for special applications.

The lack of communication between the technical field and institutions remains a formidable obstacle. Both institutions and industry are interested in a dialogue, but there is no common language. It cannot be emphasized enough that if institutions fail to communicate their needs to the hardware and software industries, they will not obtain the tools they need for their special applications. Archives and libraries should know that they are involved in creating the new standards. Today, it seems that whoever is first on the market with a new product is creating a *de facto* standard for competitors. Furthermore, time to create new standards is very short; industry will not wait years to introduce a product simply because people cannot agree on a certain issue.

A digital project cannot be looked at as a linear process in which one task follows another. Rather, it must be viewed as a complex structure of interrelated tasks in which each decision has an influence on another one. The first step in penetrating this complex structure is to thoroughly understand each single step and find metrics to quantify it. Once this is done, the separate entities can be put together in context. We are still in the first round of this process, but with the benefit of experience gathered from various digital projects, we are reaching the point where we can look at the complex system as a whole.

Sources

Arms, Caroline, ed. *Enabling Access in Digital Libraries*. Washington, DC: Council on Library and Information Resources, 1999.

Ester, Michael. *Digital Image Collections: Issues and Practice*. Washington, DC: Commission on Preservation and Access, 1996.

Frey, Franziska. "Digital Imaging for Photographic Collections: Foundations for Technical Standards," *RLG DigiNews* (December 1997). [Online] www.rlg.org/preserv/diginews

Frey, Franziska and James Reilly. *Digital Imaging for Photographic Collections: Foundations for Technical Standards* (November 1999). [Online] www.rit.edu/~661www1/sub_pages/frameset2.html

Frey, Franziska and Sabine Süsstrunk. "Color Issues to Consider in Pictorial Image Data Bases." *Proceedings IS&T's Fifth Color Imaging Conference*, pp. 112-15. Scottsdale, AZ, November 17-20, 1997.

———. "Image Quality Issues for the Digitization of Photographic Collections." *Proceedings IS&T's 49th Annual Conference*, pp. 349-53. Minneapolis, MN, May 19-24, 1996.

Gann, Robert G. *Desktop Scanners*. Upper Saddle River, NJ: Prentice Hall, 1999.

Holm, Jack. "Factors to Consider in Pictorial Digital Image Processing," *Proceedings IS&T's 49th Annual Conference*, pp. 298-304. Minneapolis, MN, May 19-24, 1996.

———. "Survey of Developing Electronic Photography Standards." *Standards for Electronic Imaging Technologies, Devices, and Systems, SPIE, Critical Reviews of Optical Science and Technology Series* 61 (1996): 120-52.

Puglia, Steve. "The Costs of Digital Imaging," *RLG DigiNews* (October 1999). [Online] http://www.rlg.org/preserv/diginews

Reilly, James. *Care and Identification of 19th-Century Photographic Prints*. Rochester, NY: Eastman Kodak Publication, 1986.

Stephenson, Christie and Patricia McClung, eds. *Delivering Digital Images—Cultural Heritage Resources for Education*. Los Angeles, CA: The Getty Information Institute, 1998.

Süsstrunk, Sabine Robert Buckley and Steve Sven. "Standard RGB Color Spaces," *Proceedings IS&T's Seventh Color Imaging Conference* (November 1999), Scottsdale, AZ.

3. An OCR Case Study

Eileen Gifford Fenton
JSTOR, University of Michigan

What is OCR?

Optical character recognition, or OCR, is the process that converts the text of a printed page to a digital file. This is accomplished by using an OCR software package to process a digital image of the printed page. The software first analyzes the layout of text on the page and divides the text into *zones* that usually correspond approximately to paragraphs. Next, the order of the paragraphs is determined and then the analysis of the characters begins. Most OCR applications work by looking at character groups, *i.e.,* words, and comparing these to a dictionary included with the application. When a match is found, the software prints the appropriate word to the text file; when a match cannot be made confidently, the software makes a reasonable assumption and flags the word as a low confidence output. Where a word or character cannot be read at all, the default character for illegible text is inserted as a placeholder.

> **Accuracy of OCR packages varies widely.**

OCR is an effective means to read modern typeface captured in high quality page images. Though OCR software has improved significantly over the last decade, OCR does not yet deal effectively with non-Arabic characters or nonmodern type and frequently struggles to translate small print, certain fonts, and complex page layouts. The accuracy of OCR packages varies widely among applications and across different source materials.

JSTOR and OCR

JSTOR, an independent not-for-profit organization headquartered in New York, NY, has the large-scale undertaking to convert and maintain digital versions of the backfiles of journals and to develop access tools that allow searching of both full text and indexed components within each issue. To date, JSTOR has converted over 4 million pages from over 100 journal titles. Over 500 academic libraries in North America and abroad have signed on as institutional participants.

JSTOR began digitizing journal back runs in the fall of 1994 with only minimal staff devoted to production activities. Since those early days both productivity levels and staffing have increased. Currently, JSTOR prepares approximately 200,000-250,000 new pages for digitization each month. The JSTOR production staff has grown to a group of 20 distributed between operations at the University of Michigan and Princeton University. Several other units at JSTOR including Library Relations, Publisher Relations, User Services, Technology Support and

Development, and an administrative group complement the work of the production group.

Each journal page digitized by JSTOR is processed by an OCR application, and the resulting text files are used to support the full text searching offered to JSTOR users. In order to ensure that search results are as accurate as possible, each OCR text file is manually reviewed and corrected to a targeted accuracy level prior to being added to the database. Eliminating this manual review could reduce production costs. However, it has proven to be an essential step for assuring both the overall quality of the database and the accuracy of scholars' full-text searches.

Key Points When Considering OCR

Digital projects vary widely in content, aim, and scale, and OCR may not be the right solution for all. When considering OCR, it is useful to weigh the following.

1) Select technology that will enhance your ability to meet the objectives of the project.

If the project goal includes delivering converted text files to the user, you will want to think very carefully about using OCR. No OCR product is perfect. Text errors will be present in files displayed to users. As a result, you will want to thoughtfully determine the

> **Manual review has proven essential.**

OCR accuracy level required to meet particular goals. If you are using the text files only to support searching, and they will not be displayed to the user, you may be able to tolerate lower accuracy. Decisions about accuracy should take into account the characteristics of the source material. Non-English text, mathematical or chemical symbols, and other special characters are not successfully translated by OCR applications, and their presence should be factored into your decision.

2) Scale matters — a lot.

The appropriate approach for generating text files is affected dramatically as you move from a 20,000-page project to a 200,000-page project to a 2,000,000-page project, even if the goals of the projects are the same. Similarly, the costs generated by text file production also change dramatically with scale.

3) There is no right answer.

Solutions will be driven by the goal of the project. However, it is difficult to generalize from one project to another even when project goals may be similar. Very specific characteristics such as the nature and quality of the source materials, the available budget, and the time allotted for the project will significantly impact decisions.

4) Costs will be higher by more than you expect.
Even the most carefully planned projects including OCR will experience surprises. Initially selected software may not perform on actual data as it did on test data. You may find processing limitations in the full production phase that were hidden during the pilot phase. Expanding an application's dictionary to include specialized terms may prove to be more difficult than originally anticipated. Any number of unexpected developments may impact production timeframes and therefore budgets. It is helpful if an allowance for these unexpected developments can be built in from the beginning of the project.

5) The answer that is right for today may not be right in the future.
OCR software capabilities have developed significantly over the last five to ten years and improvements continue to be made. The dynamic nature of this technology means that projects of more than just a few months' duration may benefit by continuing to evaluate new products as they become available to determine if greater cost-benefit possibilities have developed.

Sources

Rice, Stephen V., George Nagy, and Thomas A. Nartker. *Optical Character Recognition: An Illustrated Guide to the Frontier.* Kluwer Academic Press: part of Kluwer International Series in Engineering and Computer Science Secs 501. 1999.

Until 1997, the Information Science Research Institute at the University of Nevada, Las Vegas, conducted an annual assessments of selected OCR products. Information on their Technology Assessment Program is available at http://www.isri.unlv.edu/info/technology/

Website: www.jstor.org Readers will find information about JSTOR's mission and history, a description of the contents of the database, and information on institutions participating in JSTOR's work. Also available is a description of our production process, technical information of general interest, and a link to a demonstration of the database.

4. Digitization of Maps and Other Oversize Documents

Janet Gertz
Columbia University Libraries

Paper maps (and other oversize documents such as architectural drawings) contain a wealth of fine details composed of graphic and textual elements. They include:

- The drawing of the location
- The use of graphic entities like elevation lines or symbols for cities of different sizes
- Printed names of countries and other features
- Color, which carries information through varied patterns and intensities.

When they are large, maps with fine details present special difficulties for digitization. There can be a huge disparity between the size of the document and the size of the smallest meaningful element that must be made visible online or in printouts. Fine detail requires high resolution scanning, and the result is very large file size. File manipulation, storage, delivery, and display all become much more complicated.

Even the mechanics of scanning are affected. Many flatbed scanners have size limitations and cannot handle large maps. Scanning may require film intermediaries such as 4x5 transparencies or single-frame microfiche, where the original object fills the body of the microfiche. Thirty-five mm slides are too small to fully capture details on large maps. When originals are not only oversized but also brittle, working from a film intermediary will put less strain on the fragile original. Some loss of quality will result because the film version is one generation removed from the original. However, fully legible images can be produced from film intermediaries, always, of course, given that the transparency or microfiche is itself carefully made and then scanned with sufficient resolution and appropriate tonality.

Scanning Parameters

Determining capture parameters follows the same rules as for other documents.
- Decide on the appropriate tonality, usually gray-scale or color. Color on most printed maps is important as a coding device, not for its precise hue as it is in art works. Nevertheless, a standard color bar should be included during scanning even when sophisticated color management is not a requirement. (For a discussion, see Ester, 1996.)
- Identify the smallest meaningful element, often a thin line.
- Determine how many pixels are needed to capture the smallest element legibly.

- Calculate the necessary resolution, often 200-300 dots per inch when scanning in 24-bit color. For a discussion of resolution and related issues, see Gertz *et al.* (1996) and Allen (1998).
- Whether the map is digitized directly or through a film intermediary, always include a ruler in the image so that dimensions and distances are unambiguous.

As an example, consider a hypothetical map two feet across and three feet long.
- The smallest textual elements are numbers less than 1 mm high that record elevations.
- The smallest meaningful elements are the thin lines used to indicate elevation.
- Ten different colors serve as codes, patterned as dots, parallel vertical and horizontal lines, and other graphic devices.

A scanned version of acceptable quality would permit users working on screen and with printouts to:
- Read the 1 mm text
- See unbroken elevation lines
- Clearly distinguish all color code patterns.

Assume a minimum of 200 dpi and 24-bit color is needed to achieve legibility of the 1-mm text and the lines and code patterns. For a map 36" wide, 200 dpi multiplies out to 7,200 dots across the surface of the map. If a film intermediary is used, then the effective resolution must be calculated as well. Effective resolution refers to resolution relative to the size of the original document. A transparency still requires 7,200 dots across the map to capture the same degree of detail. The map on the transparency is perhaps only 4" wide. It must be scanned at 1,800 dpi to get the same level of detail.

To calculate the file size, use the formula given in Kenney and Chapman (1996), p. 20.

formula:	(height	x	width	x	bit depth	x	dpi^2	)	/	8
original map:	(24"	x	36"	x	24	x	200^2	)	/	8 = 103,680,000
transparency:	(2.667"	x	4"	x	24	x	1800^2	)	/	8 = 103,680,000

The product of digitizing oversize documents is clearly a series of very large files. This has implications for the image creator in terms of storage, retrieval, and display. Large files take up a great deal of storage space. Enough memory must be available for images to be loaded and manipulated. Backing up files, creating derivatives, and transmitting files absorb a significant amount of time and storage media.

Handbook For Digital Projects

Problems of Access to Scanned Large Maps

The nature of these files also translates into problems for users trying to access and navigate within digital images of large maps.

- The high-resolution image in which all of the details are visible is too big for users to access or manipulate easily, given current delivery mechanisms and the capacity of common computers.
- When derivatives of the original high-resolution files are provided for access, they are often JPEG versions with considerably reduced resolution. If the resolution is low enough to make files easy to access, the finer details in the images may become illegible.
- Only part of the map image fits on screen at one time. When using the paper document, readers orient themselves to salient features through peripheral vision while focusing closely on details. On screen, it is easy to become disoriented because most of the image is not visible.
- With a paper map, it takes a single glance to follow features such as roads or boundaries from one edge to the other, but on screen it takes continued scrolling. Comparing widely separated details becomes awkward at best if they are not visible simultaneously.

Benefits of Scanning Large Maps

Despite these difficulties, there are a variety of ways to benefit from scanning large maps.

- Use the high-resolution images to produce high quality printouts to replace brittle originals.
- Derive lower resolution versions from the high-resolution master images to serve as reference-quality images and reduce unnecessary handling of brittle originals.
- Put the images on CDs and view them directly rather than trying to deliver them over a network. The workstation must be capable of handling the large files.
- Scan large maps in sections to generate a group of high-resolution files of manageable size. This entails use of software packages for managing the separate files and concatenating them as the user moves from one to the next. It also can complicate the creation of high-resolution printouts.
- Investigate some of the new compression software that permits the user to access a lower resolution image and then zoom into higher resolutions without manipulating the whole high-resolution file locally. One such product is Lizardtech's Multi-Resolution Seamless Image Database (see http://www.lizardtech.com); a number of other packages are available.

In Conclusion

- The size of the original, in proportion to the size of the smallest meaningful element, determines the needed resolution.
- File size governs the ability to store, retrieve, and display an image.
- Excellent images will fail to satisfy users if they cannot be accessed or if equipment and software are not well suited to working with large images. Speed and smoothness of scrolling and zooming are important.
- Planning the user interface must be part of initial project design.

To view a selection of approaches to scanned maps, see:
- American Memory project:
  http://memory.loc.gov/ammem/gmdhtml/gmddigit.html
- British Columbia Archives and Records Service:
  http://www.bcars.gs.gov.bc.ca/cartogr/general/maps/html
- Library of Virginia: http://image.vtls.com/BPW
- University of Connecticut: http://magic.lib.uconn.edu/magic/exhibits/
- Atlantic Neptune: http://mercator.cogs.nscc.ns.ca/neptune.html
- National Oceanic and Atmospheric Administration:
  http://chartmaker.ncd.noaa.gov/ocs/text/MAP-COLL.htm/
- David Rumsey Associates: http://www.davidramsey.com

Sources

Allen, David. "Creating and Distributing High Resolution Cartographic Images," *RLG DigiNews* 2:4, 1998.
http://lyra.rlg.org/preserv/diginews/diginews2-4.html#feature

Ester, Michael. *Digital Image Collections: Issues and Practice.* Washington, DC: Commission on Preservation and Access, 1996.

Gertz, Janet, Robert Cartolano, and Susan Klimley. *Oversize Color Images Project,* Columbia University, 1996. http://www.columbia.edu/dlc/nysmb/

Kenney, Anne, and Stephen Chapman. *Digital Imaging for Libraries and Archives.* Ithaca, NY: Department of Preservation and Conservation, Cornell University Library, 1996.

5. Working with Microfilm

Paul Conway
Yale University Library

Preservation microfilm can be an excellent source-medium for digital conversion projects if certain caveats are taken into consideration. This section describes what librarians and archivists need to know about working with existing microfilm to produce high-quality digital images that can be displayed as images and/or processed with OCR conversion software.

Background — Project Open Book

Microfilm has been used as a medium for preservation and access since the 1930s. By the middle of the 1980s, international standards fully defined the archival qualities of preservation microfilm (Fox, 1996). The Research Libraries Group, working in close association with the American Library Association, established procedures for creating film that meets or exceeds archival standards (Elkington, 1992). By the end of 1999, the National Endowment for the Humanities had provided partial support for the preservation of over 800,000 brittle volumes on microfilm. The nation's collection of preservation microfilm is the first and one of the largest *virtual libraries* in the world (Conway, Selecting, 1996).

In the early 1990s, Don Willis, one of the most prominent experts on the creation of preservation microfilm, proposed that it was technologically and economically feasible to create high-quality digital images from microfilm (Willis, 1992). At the time he wrote, few people outside the commercial sector — and no U.S. archivists or librarians — were in a position to test the hypotheses that Willis proposed. The conversion of microfilm was largely confined to corporations that needed to convert *legacy files* from microfilm (typically, case files and standard office documents) on a highly selective basis. What was needed was a systematic exploration of the issues associated with tapping the content of hundreds of thousands of brittle books, newspapers, and serials preserved on 35 millimeter microfilm now housed in research libraries and archives around the country. If it proved feasible to obtain high quality images at a reasonable cost from the nation's corpus of preservation film, then this material could be added to what was then expected to be a national digital image resource.

Yale University Library, with the assistance of the Commission on Preservation and Access and the National Endowment for the Humanities, accepted the job of developing a sequence of projects, collectively termed Project Open Book, to test Don Willis's hypotheses (Waters, 1991). Yale designed and implemented Project Open Book in close association with Cornell University, which at the time was also deeply engaged in digital imaging R&D, using books as the principal conversion source. Yale adopted Cornell's recommendations for base line image quality and then went on to develop a complex cost study to test the underlying economic assumptions of the imaging process. Project Open Book defined the relationship between quality and cost. The project established rules of thumb for maximizing quality and baseline cost estimates for the microfilm conversion process (Conway, "Yale," 1996).

Since the Yale project has been completed, additional projects have contributed to the general microfilm-scanning knowledge base. Additionally, several service bureaus have begun offering conversion services to libraries and archives. These commercial organizations are able to meet or exceed quality expectations at a cost-per-image that is not as low as the benchmarks identified by Yale, yet still fairly cost effective. In 1999, the principal investigators of the Cornell and Yale projects pooled their knowledge of the hybrid approach and developed a set of recommendations for converting brittle books from either film or the original item (Chapman, Conway & Kenney, 1999). Together, these developments make it possible to recommend best practices for certain kinds of materials on film and to identify when microfilm is not the best source.

Image Quality Considerations

Image quality is the first concern. High contrast 35-mm microfilm, produced according to ANSI/AIIM specifications to a Quality Index level of at least 5 (on a scale of 1 to 8) has the equivalent digital resolution of at least 800 dots per inch (dpi). It is not yet possible (nor may it be necessary) to achieve this level of scanning across the full width of the 35 mm microfilm frame. High resolution scanning from microfilm varies from 300 to 600 dpi. Bit depth ranges from bitonal (1 bit per pixel) to full gray (8 bits per pixel). Scanners for color roll film (a relative rarity in libraries) are not available commercially, although such technology is an important part of the movie industry (Kenney & Chapman, 1996).

Because of the high risk of damage, master microfilm negatives (1N) should never be used as a scanning source. Research at Yale and in Germany has shown that the same level of image quality can be obtained from a duplicate negative (2N) without placing the master negative in jeopardy (Weber, 1997). If only a positive use copy (3P) is available, it is possible to obtain a readable digital image, although some detectable drop-off in image quality should be expected.

Characteristics of the original source document and characteristics of the microfilm medium strongly influence the quality of the individual images and the total image product. Here are some highlights.

Characteristics of the Original Source
(*e.g.*, book, document, print, map)

- High contrast between text (ink) and surface (paper) yields best results

- Discolored, damaged, uneven edges of paper complicate scanner setup

- Bleed-through of text from verso limits threshold options

- Foxing, mold, stains, and fire and water damage may be accentuated by scanning

- Tight gutters in bound volumes distort film and digital imagery unless corrected

- Fold-outs and oversize inserts may not be represented in digital form as accurately as baseline document (in-line modifications to scanner setting are required)

Characteristics of the Microfilm

Image Quality

- Polarity: negative microfilm yields higher quality images than positive film

- Density: medium contrast (dMax ca. .90) to high contrast (dMax ca. 1.30) film results in higher quality images than low contrast (dMax ca. .80) negatives. RLG dMin guideline (< .25) holds.

- Reduction ratio: lower is better; accurate recording of ratio is crucial for reproduction at original size

- Skew: minimize or eliminate — no greater than 5 degrees from parallel

Product Quality

- Consistent placement: minimize or eliminate *centerline weaving*

- Duplicate images: duplicate images bracketing illustrations have minimal impact

- Splices: eliminate splices inside a given volume on the reel

- Dimensions of original: record accurately on bibliographic target

- Blank frames: eliminate or reduce quantity wherever possible

- Orientation: A2 position provides most consistent product with some scanners; one full frame per image is generally preferable.

- Test charts: incorporate RIT Alphanumeric Test Chart into scanner setup routines

Conversion Cost Issues

Imaging costs are driven by scanner pricing structures, labor costs, and the overall speed of the conversion system. The throughput speed of a given scanner is a product of at least three factors:

- Image resolution (the lower the resolution the faster the output)
- Electrical engineering (fast refresh rate of the CCD array and fast data transfer rate equals fast output)
- Mechanical engineering (more rigorous film transport mechanisms provide for quicker throughput).

It is somewhat difficult to compare scanner speeds by studying manufacturer specifications.

In its complex study, Project Open Book examined the cost of the imaging process in terms of equipment and human resources (Conway, *D-Lib Magazine*, 1996). The cost model factored in the actual costs of hardware, software, integration support, and optical storage media and then converted these costs to a range of per-book and per-image costs. Most importantly, the Yale study assessed costs for each of the processing steps of the conversion process.

The Yale study identified a number of factors that contribute to variation in costs, including the following:

- The impact of original source and microfilm characteristics varies among process steps.
- Most time-consuming conversion steps (scanning in continuous mode, indexing, scanner setup, and file transfer) are not greatly influenced by original source or microfilm factors.
- Original source characteristics influence costs more than microfilm characteristics.
- Original source and microfilm characteristics, combined, have dramatic impact on quality but only marginal impact on costs.
- Pre-scan inspection of microfilm (a relatively inexpensive processing step) is an important mechanism for predicting quality control challenges, but is not sufficient for identifying significant scanning and indexing complexities that arise during the conversion process.

- Characteristics of the original source that have a large impact on quality (*e.g.*, faded text, bleed through) have little impact on the cost of digital conversion.

- The number of pages in the chunk of material being scanned has a significant financial impact on all conversion processes.

- Books without tables of contents or page numbers pose significant indexing challenges (and thus higher costs), but also complicate prescan inspection and all aspects of quality control.

- The presence of illustrations is only one of many factors that combine to explain variation in the cost of the most time-consuming processing steps.

- The costs of quality control processes carried out during scanning, indexing, and final acceptance are strongly influenced by original source characteristics (*e.g.*, tight gutter margins, cropped text, illustrations).

- Preparation of a bound volume prior to microfilming (*e.g.*, disbinding, careful cropping) can significantly reduce the cost of setting scanner parameters.

Characteristics of the Microfilm

- Reduction ratio is the single most important microfilm characteristic influencing costs. The smaller the ratio the lower the conversion cost.

- Skewed microfilm images, an all-too-common factor, increase the cost of scanning, quality control, and inspection.

- Splices inside a given volume influence the cost of several important steps, but occur too infrequently to matter much.

- The cost-per-item of scanner set up is not influenced by any characteristics of microfilm.

- Density variation has no impact on the cost of conversion.

- Investment in better quality microfilm has only marginal cost-reduction benefits.

Service Bureaus

Vendors can do the hard work. It is not necessary to purchase microfilm scanning hardware and software for in-house use in order to accomplish the conversion of microfilm. A number of companies in the United States offer conversion services, including:

- Preservation Resources of Bethlehem, PA
  <http://www.oclc.org/oclc/presres/index.htm>
- Northern Micrographics of La Crosse, WI
  <http://normicro.com>, and
- microMedia Imaging Systems, Inc. of Lake Success, NY.

Two sources for information on service bureaus are:

- *Imaging Magazine* <http://www.imagingmagazine.com> and the Association for Information and Image Management (AIIM) <http://www.aiim.org>. You must be a member ($125 individual) to take advantage of AIIM's excellent library and referral services.

It is very important to test the products (*deliverables*) of a service bureau before finalizing a contract. Most service bureaus will conduct scanning tests for free or for a modest fee as part of a competitive bidding process. It is your responsibility to specify the quality level of the digital images in terms of resolution, dynamic range (bit depth), and postscan image processing (*e.g.,* deskew, despeckle, and tone adjustment). It is also your responsibility to specify whether it is acceptable for the vendor to use equipment that uses synthetic resolution tools to offset the resolution limitations of the equipment. Finally, it is also your responsibility to specify the characteristics of the output files in terms of file format, naming conventions and directory structures, and delivery mechanism (*e.g.,* CD-ROM, FTP server, magnetic tape).

Equipment Options

If you are working with a contractor to accomplish your imaging goals, it will not be necessary to purchase scanning equipment. Nevertheless, you can and should learn as much as you can about the capabilities of scanning equipment by contacting the manufacturers of hardware and software systems.

Hardware/software capabilities must be understood in order to develop quality and cost specifications, regardless of whether a scanning program is carried out in the library. Scanning results will vary across machines, however, depending on how the software for a given machine defines the thresholds (analogous to contrast settings on a photocopier), sets the various filter options, and applies various algorithms that interpret and adjust pixel encoding. The more that is known about how the scanner interprets and codes what it sees, the better the resulting images. Ultimately, quality specifications, technology capabilities, and the visual characteristics of the original source combine to determine the quality and cost of the image product.

The following five companies either manufacture or resell four systems for microfilm scanning in the United States. In general, hardware and software are bundled as a single package. The amount of customization that can be specified by the buyer for either hardware or software varies from none (Minolta) to extensive (Amitech). The amount of end-user control over the equipment also varies widely. It is important to view and test equipment in real-world settings before purchasing equipment. The best way to undertake this testing is to ask hardware companies for a short list of client-references in the area and then contact these references directly.

Amitech Corporation <http://www.amitech.com>
5501 Backlick Road
Suite 200
Springfield, VA 22151
Phone: 703-256-2020 Fax: 703-256-9153
Amitech resells three of the four microfilm scanners (Mekel, SunRise, Wicks & Wilson) that are presently available and also provides a variety of software packages (customizable) that control the scanner operation and carry out various postscan data management tasks (*e.g.,* deskew, despeckle, compression).

Mekel Engineering, Inc. <http://www.mekel.com>
2800 Saturn Street, Suite B
Brea, CA 92821-6201
Phone: 714-996-5600 Fax: 714-996-5696
The Mekel M500 is the premier high-speed microfilm conversion product. It is capable of handling 35 mm or 16-mm roll film. The Mekel M560 is the associated hardware for fiche scanning.

Minolta Corporation <www.minolta.com>
101 Williams Drive
Ramsey, NJ 07446
Phone: 800-964-6658
Minolta manufactures the MS 3000 Microform Scanner, which can handle a full suite of formats if the transport mechanism is changed. The scanner is highly automated and provides limited operator flexibility.

SunRise Imaging, Inc. <http://www.sunriseimg.com>
1250 N. Tustin
Anaheim, CA 92807
Phone: 714-632-2160 Fax: 714-632-2161
The SunRise ProScan III is the most complex and comprehensive microfilm scanner on the market. It converts in both bitonal and gray scale mode and can handle a variety of formats depending on the configuration of the film support mechanisms.

Wicks & Wilson, Inc. <http://www.amitech.com>
Morse Road Basingstoke
Hampshire RG226PQ England
Phone: 011441256842211
The Wicks & Wilson 4000 and 4001 Scanstations are the newest arrivals to the U.S. market. They are manufactured in England by a company that specializes in high-tech imaging applications, such as virtual reality gloves. At publication time, the WW machines are available only through Amitech. The manufacturer claims high-resolution scanning and ease of use are key features.

Further Research Needed

Research needs to be done to certify the feasibility of converting nonbook materials, especially newspapers and manuscripts. Additionally, the challenges of working with microfilm that has not been created with rigorous archival standards are not well understood, including:
- Older film
- Scratched or damaged film
- 16 mm film
- Continuous tone film
- Positive polarity film
- Third generation film.

Conclusion

In the past decade, microfilm-scanning technology has matured to the point where you have distinct options regarding hardware and software capabilities, as well as choices about the quality of the end products and the cost of the technology. Quality is increasing; per-image costs are declining. You should have confidence that the digital image conversion of primarily text-based materials from preservation microfilm is both technically feasible and economically competitive with other conversion technologies.

Sources

Chapman, Stephen, Paul Conway, and Anne R. Kenney. *Digital Imaging and Preservation Microfilm: The Future of the Hybrid Approach for the Preservation of Brittle Books.* Washington, DC: Council on Library and Information Resources, 1999. [Online] Available: ttp://www.clir.org/programs/cpa/hybridin-tro.html#description

Conway, Paul. "Selecting Microfilm for Digital Preservation: A Case Study from Project Open Book." *Library Resources & Technical Services* 40 (January 1996): 67-77.

———. "Yale University Library's Project Open Book: Preliminary Research Findings," *D-Lib Magazine* (February 1996) [Online]. Available: http://www.dlib.org/magazine.html

———. *Conversion of Microfilm to Digital Imagery: A Demonstration Project.* New Haven, CT: Yale University Library, 1996.

Conway, Paul and Shari Weaver. *The Setup Phase of Project Open Book.* Washington, DC: Commission on Preservation and Access, June 1994. [Online]. Available: http://www.clir.org/pubs/reports/conway/conway.html.

Elkington, Nancy, ed. *RLG Preservation Microfilming Handbook.* Mountain View, CA: The Research Libraries Group, Inc., 1992.

Fox, Lisa, ed. *Preservation Microfilming: A Guide for Librarians & Archivists,* 2nd ed. Chicago: American Library Association, 1996.

Kenney, Anne R. and Stephen Chapman. *Digital Imaging for Libraries and Archives.* Ithaca, NY: Cornell University Library, 1996.

Waters, Donald J. *From Microfilm to Digital Imagery.* Washington, DC: Commission on Preservation and Access, June 1991.

Waters, Donald J. and Shari Weaver. *The Organizational Phase of Project Open Book*. Washington, DC: Commission on Preservation and Access, September 1992.
http://www.clir.org/pubs/reports/openbook/openbook.html/openbook.html

Weber, Hartmut and Marianne Dorr. *Digitization as a Method of Preservation? Final Report of a Working Group of the Deutsche Forschungsgemeinschaft.* Washington, DC and Amsterdam: Commission on Preservation and Access and European Commission on Preservation and Access, 1997.

Willis, Don. *A Hybrid Systems Approach to Preservation of Printed Materials.* Washington, DC: Commission on Preservation and Access, 1992.
http://www.clir.org/pubs/reports/willis/index.html

6. Cooperative Imaging: Scans Well with Others

Steven D. Smith
Editor, Microform and Imaging Review and former Imaging Service Coordinator, Amigos Library Services Inc.

Digital imaging technology can assist libraries, archives, and museums in achieving a level of cooperation never before possible. Institutions traditionally have cooperated in filling voids within local collections — microfilming archives and offering them for sale, supplying missing journal issues, and, most obviously, participating in interlibrary loan. However, digital imaging offers the ability to create virtual collections from items held at a number of geographically disparate institutions. It also enables a single network interface, allowing researchers access to materials without concern for their physical location. Cooperative projects using digital imaging also can link primary source materials together with secondary resources to provide users with a strong collection capable of satisfying the requirements of all but the deepest research.

What is Cooperative Digital Imaging?

Cooperative imaging can take a number of forms. At its most basic, cooperative projects have consisted of institutions pooling resources to purchase an imaging workstation(s) for use by all participants, or to use their aggregate buying power to secure lower per-image conversion costs from service bureaus. Another possibility is for institutions to scan and network images independently but provide a single access point for all collections (a large-scale example is the Association of Research Libraries [ARL] Digital Image Database http://www.arl.org/did/).

The type of cooperation most often associated with digital imaging creates the virtual collections described above. Examples include Research Libraries Group's Studies in Scarlet project (http://www.rlg.org/scarlet/sis.html) and the Library of Congress' American Memory project (http://memory.loc.gov/ammem/). In both cases, lead organizations provided the leadership and guidelines (and even partial funding), and contribution of collections was opened to libraries and archives across the country. Although these examples represent the efforts of the large research libraries, the activity is open to libraries, museums, and historical societies with all sizes and types of collections. In fact, the advantages of cooperation for small institutions may be greater than for larger research libraries.

Why Cooperate?

The main and obvious reason for cooperation is to provide users with enhanced access to collections. But there are additional reasons that benefit the institutions themselves. Cooperation offers opportunities to:

■ Share expertise
■ Save costs on conversion
■ Increase opportunities for funding
■ Heighten visibility for the collections by linking with similar collections and to other institutions.

Perhaps the biggest selling point for smaller institutions is the ability to share expertise. Several institutions can work together to solve problems of converting paper- and film-based collections to a digital format and networking these collections, along with the attendant problems of cataloging and creating metadata.

How Does Cooperation on Digital Imaging Differ from Cooperative Microfilming Projects?

The biggest difference between microfilming and digital imaging projects is complexity. In addition, there are established procedures and standards for microfilming, whereas we are still learning about optimal digitizing methods (hence this publication). Preservation microfilming, while requiring the participation of selectors and catalogers, is largely an undertaking of preservation reformatting staff. Selector and cataloger expertise and involvement is certainly necessary, but such folks are not asked to do anything out of the ordinary. Digital imaging requires an altogether wider level of participation from every institution, involving more involvement from a variety of staff, especially the inclusion of systems personnel.

In addition, digitization projects are not as fixed as microfilming, where the end product is essentially just cataloged and shelved. Imaging projects are not completed with the creation of digital images and their associated metadata (a complex issue in and of itself). The technical and administrative issues of networking and providing access are legion, and they must be considered and resolved before the first page hits the platen.
■ Will the images be available via the Internet?
■ How will rights be managed?
■ Will computer-searchable text be provided along with the images of textual items?
■ Who is responsible for maintaining access to the images?
■ Who owns the aggregate collection of digital images?

But digital imaging can result in a more useful end product than microfilming — one that allows simultaneous access to collections by multiple users.

In addition to the benefits discussed above, cooperative projects increase the chances of obtaining outside funding, as many grant agencies have demonstrated a preference for coordinated, multi-institution projects. Cooperative projects may actually prove less expensive (*i.e.,* more cost effective) on a per-image basis, as many of the costs relating to imaging are not so dependent on the number of images or participants and, if outsourcing, the conversion cost per image can be less.

From the standpoint of the user, cooperative projects are more likely to produce a desirable end product, both in terms of content (using the most relevant items from several collections) and form (benefiting from shared expertise, database design, intellectual access, web interface, and so forth). This is especially true for smaller institutions, where by pulling together or working with larger institutions their collections can become more useful to the researcher.

Concluding Thoughts — or How NOT to Cooperate

There are many examples of successful cooperative imaging projects: Studies in Scarlet, American Memory, the Colorado Digitization Project (http://coloradodigital.coalliance.org/), and the various implementations of Making of America (see, for example, http://moa.cit.cornell.edu/MOA/moa-mission.html and http://sunsite.berkeley.edu/moa2/). Much can be learned from these examples, but it is also worth considering those projects that fail to get off the ground — or to move from planning to implementation.

The most common causes of such failure include the reluctance to commit resources (especially staff, and especially staff with the technical expertise), the desire to wait for industry standards to appear before moving forward, and the failure to define project objectives. Digital imaging is a resource- intensive activity and cannot be undertaken without the commitment of staff. Waiting for standards to appear is no reason to hesitate. Although there are few standards relating to digitization, it must be recognized that best practices and other guidelines are appearing.

Particularly difficult with cooperative projects is the last point: developing firm project objectives. Many institutions are interested in undertaking imaging because it is a hot activity. They are only able to state a project's purpose in vague and unmeasurable terms related to improved access. For a project to be successful, it must have firm, quantifiable objectives.

On a broader level, cooperative imaging projects fail because planners have yet to establish independently what role imaging will play within their own institution. Institutions need to confront the complexities of and the myriad issues raised by digital imaging — networking, metadata applications, database creation and maintenance, rights, reference services for networked users — before a project is planned. Although it is unlikely that such issues can be resolved before a project can begin, they must be understood by all parties before moving forward.

When all is said and done, a cooperative project may seem on the surface to complicate an already complicated activity. But cooperation offers the considerable advantage of bringing together a larger number of experts with greater and more varied knowledge and experience than a single institution could ever field, thus increasing the chances of success.

One final reminder: Although the examples cited above involve some of the largest libraries in the country, cooperative imaging is open to institutions of any size. In fact, smaller institutions have much to gain from cooperation and much to offer. In brittle books microfilming, the best or only copy of an item is often located outside of the participating research libraries. The same is true with digital projects. Small and medium-sized libraries, as well as specialized libraries such as museum or medical libraries, have much to contribute when it comes to archives, manuscripts, photographs, serials, and other desirable materials. Whether participation is decided by geographic proximity, library type, or simply by joining with other institutions with similar or sympathetic holdings, all institutions can take part in an activity that brings collections together to a degree never before possible.

Summary of Key Points

- Define scope of project, including appropriate collections and level of indexing.
- Define roles of participating institutions.
- Define areas of responsibility for each institution.
- Establish measurable objectives to evaluate success of project upon completion.
- Agree on long-term maintenance of digital images and associated metadata.

VIII
Vendor Relations

Janet Gertz
Columbia University Libraries

Introduction

Quality digital conversion work can be accomplished in-house or through vending out to service providers. Regardless of whether digitization is intended to serve preservation goals, it is a waste of time and money to do a poor job. A digitally converted version of a document must be fully functional. If what is digitized is illegible or so poorly indexed that end users cannot find what they need or read it when they do find it, there is a failure to provide both preservation and access.

In order for digitization to be successful, it is essential that the institution have a clear understanding of its goal for digitization and what kind of final product will serve that goal. Understanding why a project is being undertaken will guide decision making, not only about image quality and user interfaces but about what work should be accomplished in-house and what work may safely be vended out. It is important to:

- Involve all the relevant participants (curators, technical experts, preservation officers) in determining the project goals and making the decisions that will shape it
- Keep a careful record of what decisions are made, and why, to prevent re-inventing the wheel when problems arise
- Document fully how and why work was accomplished both in-house and by the vendor in order to aid future preservation of the digital resources themselves.

There will always be an in-house component to any digitization operation. The institution that holds the materials to be digitized must take responsibility for:

- Selecting materials to be converted
- Determining the purpose of digitization and the nature of the desired product
- Establishing necessary quality levels
- Verifying the quality of the completed work.

There are arguments in favor of working entirely in-house and arguments for employing service bureaus. The difference lies in:

- The degree of immediate control over the work
- The variety of activities that can be performed
- Efficiency
- Economics.

Librarians and archivists are still learning what the parameters of high quality scanning should be. Few guidelines are in place, the vocabulary is not shared industry-wide, and it is not familiar to many librarians and archivists in any case. Institutions must experiment as they go along, and there is a steep learning curve for the institutions as well as for potential vendors. Relatively few scanning vendors work with libraries and archives. Most work routinely for organizations that want quick, cheap scanning and know little about preservation and the importance of high-quality, high-resolution images, and rich metadata. Luckily, the situation is improving and there are now a number of vendors with relevant experience who are willing to share their technical expertise.

Existing best practice and recommendations for preservation-quality resolution and tonality, based on the size of the smallest meaningful element of the document to be scanned, are laid out in earlier chapters. It also has been made clear in those chapters that every change of genre, format, and medium to be digitized introduces a host of decisions on resolution, tonality, metadata, storage media, and user presentation. There are no simple answers, and the interactions among various factors may have unexpected repercussions down the road. It can be difficult to determine which outcome is best for preservation and access purposes, and which set of procedures and technologies will provide that outcome. The lack of clear, nationally accepted standards and specifications could make it difficult to explain to vendors what level of quality is needed in order to achieve results that will be acceptable. Yet, when working with vendors, the institution must be able to state its requirements in clear, quantifiable, and verifiable instructions, and it must be able to recognize whether the product returned by the vendor is what was requested.

Why Digitize In-House

The primary argument for digitizing in-house is that it gives the institution close control over all procedures, handling of materials, and quality of products. There is no need to send valuable or fragile originals off-site and no worry about working with a vendor who turns out to be incompetent, provides something other than what was required, or goes out of business.

Working in-house is a good way to learn the technical side of digitization thoroughly — useful even when most work in future will be sent to vendors. If it is not clear what sort of product would be best, working in-house provides a way to experiment on a small scale without the need to go through writing technical specifications and contracts. A small in-house pilot can serve as a prelude to vending out the bulk of the work. In-house work on a pilot project to try out a variety of approaches may not be efficient, but it is often a necessary step in the learning process.

Working in-house is probably most successful when:
- A project is relatively small scale and easily handled within any time limits, or can be broken down into small segments;
- The institution has skilled staff, or staff with real interest and incentive to learn, and support from the administration for in-depth training;
- The institution already has appropriate equipment or funding to acquire it. (But remember that equipment and software become obsolete at a frightening pace.)

Why Use Vendors

The primary benefits of working through vendors are financial and technical.
- The institution does not have to devote space to scanning, nor does it need to convert its space (possibly including construction) to suit electrical and other technical requirements.
- The institution does not constantly need to purchase the latest equipment and software. The vendor is responsible for keeping up with the times.
- The institution does not have to deal with hiring, training of sophisticated specialist skills, and management of staff.
- The vendor and not the institution copes with costly equipment breakdowns, downtime, and correction of errors.
- The institution benefits from the vendor's economies of scale and high productivity.
- Finally, the price is stated up front.

Many institutions do not own appropriate scanning equipment, and few institutions have sufficient budgets to keep pace with the latest equipment and software coming on the market. Further, there is often no one on staff with much production-level scanning experience, and it takes time and (unfortunately) learning through failure to build up experience. In theory at least, vendors can be expected to keep up with the latest hardware and software and to have fully trained specialist staff. They also should have a very good idea of what services they can offer and what it costs to provide them.

The downside is that the institution is at a distance from the work. Careful quality control assurance by the institution becomes an essential. No one should take for granted that work is being done as specified without verification through detailed inspection of the vendor images and files.

Although working with vendors usually entails sending materials — or film intermediaries — to a service bureau located somewhere outside the institution, some vendors may be able and willing to bring in equipment to carry out scanning on site. This offers some of the benefits of in-house work, *e.g.,* original materials need not travel, closer oversight of the vendor work. But it also includes some of the deficits, *e.g.,* the need to provide an appropriate work area, day-to-day scheduling issues, security, and insurance.

How to Choose Services and Vendors

Vendors are definitely not all equal. Even when using the same equipment and methods, some vendors produce a much better product than do others. Good vendors are really interested in learning what is important to fulfilling the institution's needs, while others may consider the project a run-of-the-mill job not worth any great effort. Still others want to sell their own proprietary systems rather than to act as a conversion service.

Identifying and selecting a vendor is not a quick or easy process, especially where large and complex projects are involved. Institutions may not need to go through every step described below, but all will need to work through the basics.

- Develop an initial concept of the project and its goals.
- Identify potential vendors.
- Send out an RFI (request for information) to explain the goals of the project clearly and to discover which vendors are interested and have ideas about how to handle it.
- Establish a project methodology and quality requirements.
- Develop a short list of vendors.
- Write an RFP (request for proposal) and send it to the short list along with samples to be scanned.
- Communicate with the vendors while they work on their responses, including site visits and meetings when possible.
- Evaluate and compare the vendors' proposals and select the best.
- Write and sign a contract.
- Work with the vendor during the project.

What are the Project Goals?

The institution must decide what it wants to have done and how. For example, is the aim of digitization a visual index to a manuscript collection, a reserve reading service, detailed reproductions of brittle books, or some combination of access and preservation goals? An institution may know what it ultimately wants to achieve without knowing how to get there. In this case, the institution can describe the desired end product to vendors and ask them to propose how to achieve it, within general guidelines. Other institutions may know in detail the specific requirements for the product in terms of resolution and tonality, file types and storage media, metadata to be recorded, and possibly even the desired type of equipment and software. In these cases, they need only locate a vendor capable of meeting those requirements.

In all cases, the institution must be able to express clearly to the vendor what it needs. This can be an iterative process:

- An RFI giving a very general description of the goals to a relatively large number of vendors
- Responses from some or all of the vendors proposing various possible approaches
- Selection of one or two approaches that seem most appropriate
- An RFP in which the acceptable approaches are spelled out in much more detail and sent to a short list of vendors
- Responses from the vendors with detailed procedural information and bids on prices.

The RFI - Request for Information

The purpose of an RFI is to gain general ideas about possible approaches and to identify potential vendors. If the institution knows what it wants as a final outcome but is not sure of the best methodology/technology/software/metadata, it can use the RFI process to gain an idea of the possibilities. This works especially well when the institution queries vendors who have significant relevant experience.

The RFI consists of:

- A brief description of the proposed project including amounts, timing, and desired outcomes
- A description of any methodology the institution has in mind
- A request to the vendors to comment on the methodology
- An invitation to suggest alternatives to achieve the same outcomes
- A request to the vendors to indicate whether they would be interested in bidding on the project.

For an RFI, it makes sense to contact as many potential vendors as look reasonably likely to be interested in the project. Their responses allow comparison of various approaches, assessment of the quality of the scanning under different circumstances, evaluation of the original assumptions about the product against the actual results, and a period of some review and possible redesign of the project.

There are many ways to identify potential vendors. One of the best is to seek recommendations from knowledgeable colleagues who have vended out work similar to what the institution intends. Reports on ongoing or completed projects may provide ideas. Attend conferences where colleagues discuss their projects and vendors present their services; check the Web sites of such institutions as the Library of Congress, the National Archives, the Research Libraries Group, and other preservation-related organizations.

The Request for Proposal (RFP)

A request for proposal (RFP), in contrast to the RFI, is designed to explain in detail to potential vendors the requirements and specifications for the project, the criteria that will be used to evaluate their proposals, and the specifics of how their bids should be presented. Writing an RFP and evaluating responses can be complex and time-consuming. Examples of documents provided by RLG and the Library of Congress are quite long and complicated (over 200 pages in one instance). Although this may discourage some institutions from even considering the process, reading through the sample documents is well worth the effort. An institution can extract from these exemplars the basic principles needed to construct its own simpler document and can adapt the language to suit its requirements rather than inventing the process from scratch. Still, it is important to allow sufficient time for writing the RFP, for vendors to consider the project carefully, and for evaluating their responses. The whole process can take several months. The good news is that the RFP can translate fairly directly into the eventual contract.

Once the institution has a good idea of the specifics of project methodology, it is time to write an RFP and send it to the short list of the vendors who appear most likely to be able to accomplish the project. The goal is to give vendors full information so that they understand what is desired and can make a reasonable cost estimate for the work. The value of an RFP process is that it elicits explicit responses that can be objectively evaluated to select the best vendor. Further, clearly stated specifications can help the institution avoid the need to accept the lowest bidder if that bidder cannot satisfy the specifications.

The RFP should be clear and explicit, with a specific technical description of the deliverables and how compliance will be evaluated. The RFP should be broad enough to allow for different vendors to propose alternative methodologies where appropriate, but specific enough to ensure that they understand the standards they are required to meet. Divide the RFP into sections that deal with technical requirements, management requirements, pricing, and references. Where possible ask the vendors to provide their responses in a standard format, to facilitate comparison of competing bids.

Contents of an RFP include:
- A description of the project in terms of the ultimate objectives
- A description of the objects to be scanned in as much detail as possible to help the vendor make an intelligent bid
- The quantity and physical nature and dimensions of the materials
- A consideration of the varying sizes of the material to be scanned. Are the materials reasonably uniform throughout? If multiple genres are included, describe each group separately.
- A description of proportions. What proportions are easy or difficult to work with?

- A consideration of the content of materials. Is there an intellectual structure to the materials that must be maintained? Will vendors be able to batch each type of material, or must materials be handled in an order that mixes different sizes and types?
- A consideration of language. What languages does the vendor need to be able to read (text or page numbers) in order to carry out the project?
- Detailed instructions about the preferred methodology, including resolution, tonality, bit depth, file formats, compression, platform, and storage media
- Instructions for producing derivative images as well as the master images
- Definition of the required level of accuracy and how the institution will evaluate it
- Instructions on file naming and metadata
- How to format file names
- Whether pre-existing identification numbers or other information must be keyed in
- What information about processing and equipment must be reported (*e.g.,* kind of scanner used, its settings, color definitions used, date of capture, description of film stock if film intermediaries are scanned)
- Requirements for how the data should be coded in and laid out, and what type of spreadsheet or database to use
- Schedule for weekly/monthly deliveries, deadlines, and turnaround time
- Handling (and lighting levels if that is an issue), security, insurance, and shipping requirements for original materials
- Name of the person at the institution the vendor should contact with questions and to whom the bid should be sent and in how many copies.

Ask vendors to:
- List the hardware and software they would use (Are files and data in proprietary systems acceptable?)
- Specify their quality control procedures
- Describe their production capacity and document that they can accomplish the work at the specified quality within the timeframe
- Explain how delivery of materials and files will be accomplished (vendor pick up, courier, UPS, or other)
- Describe environmental controls in the facility if that is an issue for original materials.
- Provide the name and qualifications of the project manager
- Supply references for similar work done with other libraries, archives, or museums
- Scan a representative sample that represents a fair cross section of the materials, including both easy and difficult items (If the originals are valuable or fragile, the sample should consist of reasonably similar items that are less valuable or are expendable.)
- Respond with a price proposal
- State prices in specified units of measure, for instance per page, per image, or whatever is appropriate

- Costs for data input, cost of storage media, shipping, insurance, and any other additional charges
- Determine if prices are firm for the duration of the project
- Provide suggestions for alternative methods that can accomplish the project at the same level of quality.

Communicating with Vendors During the RFP Process

Expect questions from the vendors as they work through the RFP. Insightful questions can help refine the project plan.

Depending on the circumstances, and especially if vendors will be scanning original materials, invite them to attend a meeting at the institution to see the materials and participate in a question session before they respond.

If possible, make site visits to see whether each vendor has the capacity and staffing to handle the work and whether the facilities are clean and well managed.

Evaluating Responses from Vendors

While writing the RFP, the institution should be building a plan for evaluating the responses and writing up criteria for objective and accurate comparison of the vendors' abilities to meet the specifications and requirements. Some people advocate setting up a numerical rating system, with higher weight given to the more important aspects of the proposal. A rating on a scale of 1-3 might be given to each factor to be evaluated, with the more important factors then multiplied by a weighting factor. Whether or not actual numerical ratings are assigned, the most important factors (sometimes called *critical success factors*) are the ones necessary for a successful project. For instance, the ability to provide a database for the metadata may be required (*critical*), while any serviceable software may be acceptable.

Write up criteria and benchmarks for evaluation of image quality and metadata accuracy. Establish how you will perform image quality evaluation; determine what viewing software, monitor, and printer will be used; and decide who will make the evaluation.

Criteria for assessing bids include:
- Quality of vendor products and technical methodology
- Appropriate overall technical approach
- Ability to produce sample work that meets or exceeds the RFP specifications
- Familiarity with existing guidelines and best practices
- Satisfactory quality control procedures
- Identification of unusual items, and judgment in asking the institution for further instructions

- Ability to handle original materials safely and house them securely
- Demonstrated understanding of the scope of work and the requirements
- Clear evidence that the vendor really understands the project
- Ability to answer all RFP questions in the terms requested. (If they can't follow instructions, will they be able to do the work properly?)
- Evidence of ability to carry out the whole project
- Size of the organization (Is the company large enough to handle the project or will it need to hire new, inexperienced staff?)
- Ability to accomplish the work within the project timeframe and schedule
- Successful previous experience with similar work
- Staff and facilities
- A bid that is professional in appearance and presentation
- Personnel with appropriate experience and a cooperative, service-oriented, professional attitude
- Up-to-date equipment and clean, well-organized facilities
- Commitment to the work and to the long-term relationship that will be necessary for a successful project
- Financially sound basis for the company
- Reasonable cost proposal.

Carry out the evaluation of the quality and technical adequacy of the responses separately from comparison of the cost proposals. Establish which of the vendors meet the criteria before determining which price is best. Eliminate any vendor who cannot meet the quality and technical criteria, regardless of the price.

Compare the RFPs and samples carefully using the established criteria. Discuss any unclear, unexpected, or unsatisfactory issues with the vendor. Consider providing a second chance if an unsatisfactory result was due to misunderstanding of the requirements.

Call the references and conduct thorough discussions of vendor quality, service attitude, turnaround, and other factors. Before calling, develop a series of questions to make sure no important issues are omitted.

Rank the vendors whose quality, workflow, technology, and facilities best meet the criteria and needs of the project.

Compare the price bids to identify the vendor with the best combination of high success scored in the evaluation of the bids and samples and low price. Beware of any bid that is priced unrealistically low (or high). Vendors are well aware of each other's prices and of their own profit margins. Vendors who propose similar work will generally fall within a range of prices (although companies that are either very small or part of a very large corporation may fall toward one extreme or the other). If any vendor's price is significantly lower, be wary. A very low bid may indicate a vendor who cuts corners or has failed to understand what is really required to achieve the final product. Very low prices can be a hint of low quality unless that vendor is much larger and more experienced than the others, is located somewhere where very low wages are paid, or is proposing a completely different solution. On the other hand, very high price is not necessarily a guarantee of very high quality — it may simply indicate over-charging.

If the low bidder is not the preferred vendor, determine whether the low bidder can meet the specifications at all based on samples, references, and bid statements. If not, this forms grounds for rejecting the bid. If no one vendor combines all desired factors, discuss possible changes with the preferred vendor(s) to bring them closer to the desiderata.

The Contract

Depending on the institution and the complexity of the work to be done, anything from a simple letter of agreement to a full contract may be required before vendor work on the project can begin. The specifications laid out in the RFP serve as the body of the agreement, to which are added logistic, legal, and financial details. Needless to say, involving the institution's financial and legal offices early in the process is recommended.

Contracts normally begin with sections covering the legal obligations of the two parties and a description of the work being contracted. Details, such as procedures, can be attached as appendices. The contract should:

- State what the project goal or product is supposed to be
- Describe briefly what the institution is responsible for sending, including original objects, film intermediaries, list of file names or a filenaming scheme
- Describe briefly what the vendor is agreeing to do, for instance, produce digital images, carry out OCR, create metadata files
- State the legal terms covering subcontracting
- Specify terms for accepting the product by defining the minimum acceptable level of accuracy
- Specify how errors will be defined and corrected, what error correction will be cost-free, and what the institution must pay for
- Specify how materials and files are to be transported and handled
- Specify insurance, security, and storage environment while materials are at vendor and in transit
- Name the primary contact on either side, and arrange for periodic visits to the site and visits from the vendor to the institution
- State that the materials and any products produced from them are the property of the institution and may not be used or distributed for any purpose without official written permission from the institution
- Specify frequency of reports and invoices and what information they must contain
- Specify deadlines and penalties for missed deadlines
- Define what will constitute default, how to dissolve the contract amicably on mutually specified grounds, and how to handle arbitration

- State the prices and guarantee that prices will remain firm for the duration or will increase only under specified conditions.

The second part of the contract lays out the technical specifications, including:
- Equipment and software to be used
- Storage media to use
- Specifications to follow for resolution, tonality, file formats, compression, and so forth
- The form in which to enter filenames and metadata
- How the vendor will carry out quality control.

Appendices cover details of:
- In-depth descriptions of the materials
- Schedule, timeline, benchmarks
- Error correction, handling of originals, shipping
- Samples of work forms
- Other useful information.

Once the contract is written to the institution's satisfaction, a common procedure is to send two copies to the vendor. The vendor will probably have changes to suggest. If negotiations result in significant changes, a new version may be needed. If the changes are small and simple, they can be written in and initialed by the vendor and the institution. Once the contract is fully settled, the vendor signs both copies and returns them to the institution. The institution signs both, and returns one copy to the vendor.

Working and Communicating with Vendors

Together with careful planning beforehand, the keys to a successful project are flexibility and constant communication with the vendor during the project. The better the communication between the institution and the vendor, the better the project is likely to go. It is important to assign responsibility for day-to-day communication to one person in the institution who is closely involved with the project, even if that person must refer some questions to others in the institution. In the same way, ask the vendor to name one person to serve as the institution's project contact. Encourage the vendor to communicate in a timely manner by telephone, fax, or email whenever issues arise, and be conscientious about responding quickly. Delays in solving a small problem can hold up the entire project. If possible, visit the vendor during the project and invite the vendor to visit the institution as well.

The essence of good vendor relations is to be fair to the vendor. Stay on schedule, or if unavoidable delays arise, inform the vendor as soon as possible and be prepared to shift the entire project schedule. Vendors schedule the work they take on fairly tightly. If delays at the institution's end push the project out of its assigned window of time, the vendor cannot slow down other institutions' work to recoup the lost time.

Maintain agreed-upon levels of productivity for shipments to the vendor and avoid unannounced changes in the nature or quality of the materials. For instance, if the vendor bids on the basis of a sample of uniformly legible and nonbrittle materials, inclusion of a significant amount of low contrast or brittle items can seriously affect the anticipated workflow and productivity. Significant increase or decrease in what the institution sends also can throw off the vendor's workflow and should be negotiated. Be sure all materials are prepared in the agreed upon manner before they are sent to the vendor. Finally, label all materials clearly and consistently so that the vendor can easily determine what is what.

Working with Vendors: Quality Control and Handling Corrections

Other chapters describe how to carry out quality control on images. Accuracy of vendor-supplied file names and metadata also must be verified, since erroneous metadata or miskeyed file names in essence mean that an image is lost. Calling up image after image and examining them carefully for flaws is a very time-consuming operation, but it is essential to ensuring that the vendor's product meets specifications.

When working with an unfamiliar vendor, it is especially important to carry out thorough quality control as early as possible in the project. Timeliness in returning errors is important, since:

- It prevents the vendor from continuing to replicate errors
- It alerts the vendor to problem procedures or ill-trained staff
- There is normally a cut-off date (often several months) after which the vendor will no longer accept errors for free correction.

With a new project some misunderstandings should be expected. Unexpected situations will arise as the institution and the vendor begin work on materials that may vary more than anticipated. Expect the first few months to be a shakedown period. There will probably be work in the first few shipments that will need to be redone. Once procedures are adjusted and initial problems are solved, the vendor should be expected to meet the institution's specifications routinely.

If the project is small it may be possible to examine every image, but most projects are too large. In this case, recommended procedures are as follows.

- Set up a manageable first shipment that will be due back at an early date in the project.
- Perform careful quality control on 100% of the images and metadata in the first returned shipment.
- Record all errors in detail on quality control worksheets.

- Evaluate the errors to determine which are the institution's responsibility due to flaws in the institution's own procedures, to information that the institution failed to give the vendor, or to variations in the materials being scanned that the vendor should have been warned of. The institution will need to pay to have these errors corrected and obviously will need to revise procedures to avoid them in future.

- Determine which errors are due to mistakes by the vendor. If the percent of errors is higher than the agreed-upon rate, return the entire shipment with a full explanation of the errors and require the vendor to start over and produce a new batch. As necessary, discuss changes in vendor procedures for image capture and quality control.

- Repeat the 100% inspection. If the error rate is still too high, send it back again to be redone completely. If the vendor cannot get it right by the third try, it may be time to renegotiate the whole project.

- If the vendor's work meets or is lower than the agreed-upon error rate, return only the individual problem cases for corrections.

- Continue 100% inspection for the first two to three shipments.

- Once it is clear that the vendor is regularly returning a product below the acceptable error rate, cut back to a lower percent (often 10%) inspection of every shipment. This does mean that a few errors will go undetected until the day some user tries to access those images.

- If the error rate begins to climb, return to 100% inspection until the problem is identified and solved.

Stick to the agreed-upon definitions for acceptable quality. If the institution decides it does not like the quality of the product but the vendor is meeting the agreed specifications, a change to higher quality levels is a matter for negotiation.

Sources

Electronic Imaging Request for Proposal Guidelines, ANSI/AIIM TR27-1996.

Sample RFI and RFP documents also can be found at:
The Library of Congress. The American Memory Project Background Papers and Technical Information site includes three National Digital Library RFPs for scanning and text conversion services. These are long, complex documents with all the bells and whistles required by a federal agency.
http://memory.loc.gov/ammem/ftpfiles.html

Research Libraries Group (RLG), Preservation Program Tools for Digital Imaging, provides a series of documents produced by Cornell University's Department of Preservation and Conservation for RLG. They include a worksheet for estimating costs, guidelines for creating an RFI and an RFP, and a model RFI and RFP. Significantly simpler than the Library of Congress examples, the models are very thorough in their coverage of the issues.
http://lyra.rlg.org/preserv/RLGtools.html

IX
Digital Longevity

Howard Besser
University of California, Los Angeles
School of Education & Information Studies

With a vast number of resources being committed to reformatting into digital form, we need to consider how we can ensure that digital information will continue to be accessible over a prolonged period of time. This chapter first outlines the general problem of information in digital form disappearing. It then looks closely at five key factors that pose problems for digital longevity. Finally, we turn our attention to a series of suggestions that are likely to improve the longevity of digital information, focusing primarily on metadata. This chapter was written for the library, museum, and archives communities. However, the observations will be useful for all communities wishing to ensure the longevity of any type of digital information.

The Short Life of Digital Information

Although the advent of electronic storage is fairly new, a substantial amount of information stored in electronic form has deteriorated and disappeared. For example, archives of videotape and audiotape, such as fairly recent interviews designed to capture the last cultural remnants of Navajo tribal elders, may not be salvageable (Sanders, 1997).

Most people tend to think that (unlike analog information) digital information will last forever, yet fail to realize the fragility of digital works. Many large bodies of digital information (such as significant parts of the Viking Mars mission) have been lost due to deterioration of the magnetic tapes on which they reside. But the problem of storage media deterioration pales in comparison with the problems of rapidly changing storage devices and changing file formats. It is almost impossible today to read files from the 8-inch floppy disks that were popular twenty years ago, and trying to decode WordStar files from a dozen years ago can be a nightmare. Vast amounts of digital information from just twenty years ago are, for all practical purposes, lost.

To prevent further loss, we need to come to grips with the problems of longevity in the digital world. We need to see how preservation in the digital world differs from what we have become accustomed to in the analog world. In the analog world, all of our efforts to preserve a work focused on that work as an artifact. As we begin to engage in preservation of information in digital form, we need to make a conceptual leap from preserving a physical object to preserving informational content that may be completely disembodied from any physical artifact.

The following sections address five key factors that pose digital longevity problems: the Viewing Problem, the Scrambling Problem, the Inter-relation Problem, the Custodial Problem, and the Translation Problem.

The Viewing Problem

Digital information created in the past requires the maintenance of an infrastructure and knowledge base in order to view it. For example, to view an older word processing file, one needs software that understands the encoding schemes of the original software and can display the file properly on the screen. Without this, all we will be able to see is gibberish. But to keep these files alive over time, we also need to keep software to run it or knowledge of the encoding scheme, and we must be able to produce software that uses the encoding scheme to properly display the digital files on the screen.

The default for digital information is not to survive ...

In the analog world, previous formats persisted over time. Cuneiform tablets, papyrus, and books all exist until someone or something (fires, earthquakes) takes action to destroy them. But the default for digital information is not to survive unless someone takes conscious action to make them persist. Oftentimes in the past, we have found old manuscripts or books squirreled away in basements or attics. The word processing files of today found in the attics or basements of the future won't be readable unless their authors take some concrete action to make them persist. Even if we can read the floppy disks that we find and discover that there are files on them, we won't likely be able to decipher those files and display them properly.

When we discover older analog works, at least we can view them and their structure even if we have lost the ability to decode their language. And the subsequent discovery of works like the Rosetta Stone allows us to decode their structure and meaning. Likewise, when we discover old film (either still or moving images), even if we don't have the right projector for that format, we can still hold it up to the light and see what's on it.

Digital information requires an elaborate set of knowledge and/or computing environment in order to decipher it. The information is usually encoded: To view it requires applications software that runs on a particular operating system and that needs a particular hardware platform. In addition, the information is usually stored on a physical device (like a hard disk drive, floppy disk, or CD-ROM) that requires a particular type of driver connected to a particular type of computer.

We're creating a Tower of Babel in the proliferation of combinations needed to view a file.

Each piece of that infrastructure is changing at an incredibly rapid rate — in a way that allows the computer industry to repeatedly sell the same type of product to the same person (because the individual supposedly needs a faster or newer version). The rapid changes in hardware and software versions create a headache for those interested in digital longevity. This includes problems with file formats, storage devices, operating systems, and hardware.

Most of today's word processors cannot read files created with older word processors. Most organizations have trouble even opening files created with the most popular word processor of only a dozen years ago (WordStar). In fact, today's popular word processors (such as Microsoft Word) cannot read files created with earlier versions of the same word processor (and often can only read files created in the most recent two versions). How can we ever hope that the files we create today will be readable in our information environments 100 years from now?

When today's word processors are able to open files from the more recent versions, often these files lose their formatting. Boldface, underlining, centering, and indentation change or disappear. But at least most of our older word processing files are primarily ASCII text interspersed with formatting commands. Attempts to resurrect such a file at least have some hope of finding words and phrases contained within it. For file formats not based upon ASCII text (such as multimedia file formats), however, there is little hope that archeologists a century from now will be able to decipher anything at all within these files. Formats such as TIFF, AVI, the various versions of MPEG, and so forth will pose even more longevity problems than word processing files.

Changing storage devices also pose problems for the future. In less than 20 years we have gone through removable storage devices including: 8" floppies, 5.25" floppies, 3.5" floppies, CD-ROMs, and DVDs. With increases in storage density, there is little hope that the movement to new storage devices will subside anytime soon. Today, when we discover an 8" floppy, we have to first find an appropriate 8" disk drive, attach that to a computer and operating system that has an appropriate driver and can read it, and after doing all of this, we still have the problems outlined above in deciphering the file format. With our changes in operating systems (CP/M, MS DOS, Windows, Windows 95, Window NT, Windows 2000) and hardware platforms (8088, 8086, 286, 386, 486, Pentium, Pentium II, Pentium III), we're creating a literal Tower of Babel in the proliferation of combinations needed to view a file.

Though digital longevity would seem to require it, how can we ever hope to deal with all these permutations and combinations? Think of all the formats we'd have to save, or all the emulations we'd need to decipher just the currently existing files.

The Scrambling Problem

In order to solve short-term problems resulting from the use of digital technology, we've engaged in practices that may result in long-term peril. Two noteworthy examples are how we have dealt with storage constraints and with digital commerce.

In the past, because large-scale storage was costly and bandwidth was fairly narrow, many repositories responded to these constraints by compressing their master images or multimedia. According to the reasoning that dominated until recently, compressed master files take up less storage, are easier to deliver to users with slow network connections, and are more convenient to handle internally. In recent years, a number of institutions have come to question this tenet as storage costs have plummeted and network speeds have dramatically increased. Yet the notion that one should compress even the master files still persists in many institutions.

Compression creates a number of problems. First, we don't yet really understand the long-term effects of compression. Compression can be *lossy* or *lossless*. By definition, when a lossless compressed image is decompressed, it is identical to the image before it was compressed. But when a lossy compressed image is decompressed, it is different from the original image because some information was eliminated as part of the compression process. Common lossy image compression formats, such as JPEG, essentially try to throw away information that is not too distinguishable to the human eye (colors that are close to one another get combined; spectral ranges beyond human perception are eliminated). But we don't yet understand whether some of this eliminated data will prove useful to future applications that will employ machine (rather than human) vision — applications that may perform functions such as color analysis, comparing and overlaying images, for example. Use of lossy compression today may preclude certain uses of these images in the future.

Another very important issue is that both lossy and lossless compression add still another level of complexity to the encoding of a file, making it even more difficult for future archeologists trying to decipher its contents.

In a similar way, a number of efforts to enhance digital commerce may pose threats to longevity. Encryption schemes to inhibit unauthorized use add a level of complexity to a file's encoding, again increasing the problem for future archeologists trying to decipher a file's contents. And it's difficult to believe that all the pieces of complex digital commerce schemes like container architecture (which rely both on encryption and on the continued existence of an authority that can approve a payment transaction and release the appropriate key to decrypt the file) will survive long enough to ensure access to a digital file for more than a decade.

Most of these scrambling schemes are proprietary, and most don't adhere to widely accepted standards. The level of complexity that scrambling adds makes it difficult to believe that anyone will be able to decode today's scrambled files even fifty years from now.

The Inter-relation Problem

In the digital world, information is increasingly inter-related to other information. The World Wide Web is a primary example of how any given work may incorporate or point to a number of other works. Frequently a given work may actually consist of more than one distinct file that may or may not be displayed as if they are a single file (such as when a user views what looks like a single display but is actually composed of a digital image residing in one file, with its title and other descriptive metadata residing within a separate file).

Today Web designers are encouraged to engage in good practice, taking advantage of the hypertext aspects of the World Wide Web by breaking up documents into small pieces, each stored in a separate file. These pieces can then be reassembled at viewing time so that they resemble the original full document, or the various pieces can be recontextualized in different forms for different purposes. This means that even simple works may consist of several files and that any given file may be part of more than one work.

On today's Web it is difficult to strive to make our own works persist when they point to and integrate with works owned by others. Because the current scheme for referencing Web files (the URL) is based upon a file's location, any time the file location changes, links break and users experience the most common error message on the Web ("404 Not Found"). Usually this problem is caused by some simple reorganization at the pointed-to Web site (the renaming of a file or of a folder/directory somewhere above it in the storage hierarchy, or the renaming of a server). But this common act of file/site management wreaks havoc on any works that point to or incorporate files from that site.

Another critical subset of the inter-relation problem is the issue of determining the boundary of a set of information (or even of a digital object). Today the boundaries of a digital work are no longer confined to a single file. Frequently, a Web page will incorporate images, graphics, and buttons that are stored in separate files (and sometimes even on separate servers managed by separate organizations). Even traditional works like a journal article, report, or essay are frequently broken up into several separate files that are either assembled together at viewing time by a user's browser, or remain separate linked files that a user must click between (for the stylistic purpose of not presenting the user with displays exceeding two screens-full in length).

If we want to take action to preserve one of these complex works, we need to develop guidelines on where the boundaries of the work lie. If a work incorporates pieces owned or managed by another organization (icons, logos, images, text), does saving a copy of those pieces raise intellectual property questions? If we want to be able to show future researchers what kind of information was organized and distributed by an organization today, should we try to save that organization's home page and every page that the home page links to? What about the pages linked to by those other pages? Where are the boundaries? This is not unlike the problem faced today by lecturers who want to demonstrate their Web site in a lecture hall not equipped with an Internet connection; they must decide how many layers of inter-related files to download onto a demonstration machine.

The Custodial Problem

Though a number of traditions have developed concerning which organizations should take responsibility for preserving and maintaining various types of analog material (correspondence, manuscripts, printed matter), no such traditions exist yet for digital material. As a result, much current material originating in digital form falls through the cracks and is unlikely to be accessible to future generations.

For example, special collections librarians who aggressively pursue print-based collection development in their particular specialty areas claim that

Definitions of Digital Longevity Terms

The key technical approaches for keeping digital information alive over time were first outlined in a 1996 report to the Commission on Preservation and Access (Task Force 1996).

- *Refreshing* involves periodically moving a file from one physical storage medium to another to avoid the physical decay or the obsolescence of that medium. Because physical storage devices (even CD-ROMs) decay, and because technological changes make older storage devices (such as 8" floppy drives) inaccessible to new computers, some ongoing form of refreshing is likely to be necessary for many years to come.
- *Migration* is an approach that involves periodically moving files from one file encoding format to another that is useable in a more modern computing environment. (An example would be moving a WordStar file to WordPerfect, then to Word 3.0, then to Word 5.0, then to Word 97.) Migration seeks to limit the problem of files encoded in a wide variety of file formats that have existed over time by gradually bringing all former formats into a limited number of contemporary formats.
- *Emulation* seeks to solve a similar problem that migration addresses, but its approach is to focus on the applications software rather than on the files containing information. Emulation backers want to build software that mimics every type of application that has ever been written for every type of file format and make them run on whatever the current computing environment is. (So, with the proper emulators, applications like WordStar and Word 3.0 could effectively run on today's machines.)

Both a migration and an emulation approach require refreshing.

it should be the responsibility of their organization's computing staff to pursue collection development of material originating in digital form ("Collecting at the Margins...," 1999). Yet those computing staff claim that it should be the subject-matter specialists' responsibility to pursue collection development of digital materials. Meanwhile, much of this fragile material is not collected at all.

Another example is correspondence, which in an analog world left a paper trail. Most organizations follow guidelines for saving significant amounts of paper-based correspondence. Few organizations have developed similar guidelines for saving electronic correspondence, and few individuals have any idea of how they might save their own personal correspondence even if they were eager to do so. This problem is becoming more acute as more and more important correspondence originates in digital form.

One final example is from the domain of literary creation. In the analog world, authors used to leave important traces of their creative process in the form of numerous drafts, marked-up manuscripts, and correspondence. Today they use word processors and email for both drafts and correspondence. Frequently, they only save a very few of their drafts and none of their correspondence.

A major question we face in the coming years is: Who should be responsible for saving material in electronic form? Should individuals carry this responsibility themselves? Or should social entities (such as businesses, libraries, archives, and professional societies) aggressively intervene to save material? And how will they decide what to save?

Another critical question is: How should they go about saving it? Our field still needs to develop guidelines and best practices so that organizations and individuals who want to make the effort to try to make digital information persist will know how to do so.

A key function of archives is ensuring the authenticity of a work. They do this by amassing *evidence* and by maintaining a *chain of custody*. But when works are subject to repeated acts of refreshing as most approaches to digital longevity propose (see Sidebar), these traditional ways of ensuring authenticity break down. Files repeatedly copied to new strata face the likelihood that changes will be introduced into these files, and we know little about how to control mutability across repeated refreshments.

The Translation Problem

When content is translated into new delivery devices (such as digital forms), the change of form often serves to change part of the meaning. Conversions from analog to analog face this problem, as do conversions from analog to digital (a photograph of a painting is not the same as that painting, and a digital representation of an object is not the same as that object) (Besser 1987).

Because we can make identical copies of digital files, some people mistakenly believe that digital-to-digital conversion will not face the same translation problems that analog-to-digital conversions face. This is not true because, though the bits in the file's contents may be identical, the applications environment used to view the file most certainly will be different. In fact, the very reason for converting the file is because we are unable to successfully sustain that application's environment over time.

Many people have experienced this as their word processor "successfully" imports a document created with an earlier version of the same word processor, while losing formatting (such as centering, underlining, and font changes) or punctuation (losing apostrophes or double-quotes). This also can be true in emulation environments because the creators of these environments choose which aspects of the environment to emulate, and they cannot possibly emulate every single aspect. (For example, a recent emulation of one of the earliest computer games *Moon Dust* was shown to its original designer [Jaron Lanier] who contended that it was a completely different game than the one he designed because the pacing was different.)

When saving a work, it is critical that we save parts of the work's environment that might not be immediately obvious. For example, anyone is likely to recognize that we must save the image of every page in a digitized book. But for the book to be useable, we also must save important behaviors of the book, such as the metadata and accompanying behaviors that will allow future users to turn pages, skip from the table of contents to a particular chapter, or go back and forth between the main body of text and citations or footnotes (Making of America II . . . , 1998). Saving just the page images of a book without its behaviors would be like saving a video game with the interactions in some kind of representation, but missing one of the most critically important functions.

With a work that starts out in digital form, we need to better understand the aspects of the work's original environment that are critical to viewing the work, and we need to figure out ways to sustain all the important behaviors of the work as we move its contents through generations of migration or emulation (Besser & Gilliland-Swetland, 1999). We also need to understand how each new viewing environment affects the nature of a work. (For example, many filmmakers would contend that their film is radically changed when shown on a video screen. How will today's multimedia creators feel about their works being shown in future environments where cathode ray tubes are no longer available for display?)

Paths to Improving Digital Longevity

Given these formidable problems, how can we hope to ensure the longevity of today's works that we want to preserve? A few of these approaches were first sketched out in 1998 (Lyman & Besser, 1998), but the information below has been informed by more recent thought and developments.

Broad Approaches

First, we need to recognize that we know a great deal about how to preserve bits over time. For more than a quarter of a century the data-processing community has moved large centralized bodies of bits from one physical storage medium to another. Our community needs to study corporate and university data processing departments to learn about their experiences and to obtain cost figures. Then we need to examine how these might be applied to the less highly centralized bodies of digital information of our community.

While studying this experience, we also need to keep in mind that preserving bits is only a small part of the problem. This problem is dwarfed by the much larger problems of ensuring that file formats will be accessible, and of problems involving organization, policy, and roles and responsibilities.

In the thousands of years since the Library at Alexandria was destroyed, redundancy has been a key to the preservation of information. The existence of multiple copies of a work geographically dispersed among a number of sites has helped preserve works from both natural and human-created disasters (ranging from fires and earthquakes to accidental obliteration of a set of works). Any long-term preservation strategy for digital information must incorporate cooperative relationships among physically dispersed locations and organizations. We need to develop international cooperative projects where organizations are willing to store and refresh redundant copies of works that are under the custodianship of other organizations.

Current intellectual property laws inhibit archives and libraries from preserving information in digital form, particularly since much of the digital information they acquire is licensed rather than owned. A recent study on copyright by the National Academy of Science (Committee on Intellectual Property Rights . . . , 2000) strongly recommended that intellectual property laws be changed to permit these institutions to legally preserve information in digital form, and that significant funding be allocated to digital preservation. We need to continue to monitor changes in intellectual property law (Besser, *Copyright* website) and press for the changes that will allow us to engage in digital preservation without facing criminal penalties.

We need more experience in the two competing strategies for digital preservation — *emulation and migration* (see Sidebar). The emulation approach is highly experimental, and we need to monitor the two experimental international studies that have recently begun to explore this area: NEDLIB, sponsored by the European Community (Networked European Deposit Library website); and the CEDARS Project (CURL Exemplars in Digital Archives website), sponsored by Britain's Joint Information Systems Committee and the U.S. National Science Foundation.

What We as a Community Can Do

Although no one has yet solved the broad set of problems around digital longevity, there are a number of particular actions we can take that will improve the likelihood that a work we seek to save will remain accessible over a prolonged period of time. There are also a series of actions that our community as a whole must begin to grapple with in order to reduce this immense problem.

Our community needs to insist upon clearly readable standardized ways for a digital object to self-identify its format and the applications needed to view it. With a standard for embedding the name of the viewing application in a particular place within an image header, 22nd century archeologists discovering today's files will at least be able to discover what applications they need to look for in order to view this file. Work on this and a number of related problems for longevity of digital images was begun as part of a Spring 1999 invitational meeting sponsored by the Commission on Preservation and Access, the National Information Standards Organization, and the Research Libraries Group (Besser, 1999).

Our community needs to better understand how information relates to other information (Besser & Gilliland-Swetland, 1999). In particular, we need further clarity about what constitutes the boundaries of information objects. When we are trying to save something (particularly a hypertext or hypermedia object), we need to know what pieces we really need to save.

Finally, our community needs to develop a concrete set of guidelines that can be used by people and organizations wishing to make information persist. In a sense, this chapter is one attempt at struggling with what might be in such guidelines.

In deciding to digitally preserve a group of works, the institution must first understand the special needs of the types of works contained in that collection. This means understanding how reformatting these into another format may affect the understandability and the usability of those works. This means understanding the boundaries of this work and which pieces must be saved (perhaps even including contextual pieces). As we saw with the example of a digitized book, this also means saving the behaviors of a work, not simply its contents.

The Role of Metadata

At this point in time, extensive metadata is our best way of minimizing the risks of a digital object becoming inaccessible. Properly used, metadata can:
- Identify the name of the work, who created it, who reformatted it, and other descriptive information

- Provide unique identification and links to organizations, files, or databases that have more extensive descriptive metadata about this work (this is particularly important in the likely event that the digital file and its external metadata become separated)

- Explain the technical environment needed to view the work, including applications and versions numbers needed, decompression schemes, other files that need to be linked to it, and so forth.

Various types of metadata that appear unimportant today may prove critical for properly viewing these files in the future. (For example, saved information about a particular scanner's color profile will be critical for future color management systems to account for display device differences and to properly display colors on a particular device.) A good rule of thumb is to save any metadata that is cheap and easy to capture, or that someone has indicated might eventually be important.

Sources

Those involved in planning for digital longevity should read the key texts that have scoped out the problems for our field: the Commission on Preservation and Access report (Task Force, 1996), the Getty's *Time & Bits* conference on digital preservation (MacLean & Davis, 1998), and other items referenced on the Sunsite Longevity Page (Besser, *Digital Longevity* website). They also can continuously monitor the Sunsite Longevity Page (Besser, *Digital Longevity* website), publications of the Commission on Preservation and Access (Commission on Preservation and Access website), and the work of the Internet Archive (Internet Archive website).

Besser, Howard. "The Changing Museum" in Ching-chih Chen, ed., *Information: The Transformation of Society*, pp. 14-19. Proceedings of the 50th Annual Meeting of the American Society for Information Science, Medford, NJ: Learned Information, Inc.

———. *Copyright* (website). http://www.gseis.ucla.edu/~howard/Copyright/

———. *Digital Longevity* (website). http://sunsite.berkeley.edu/Longevity/

———. Image Metadata: meeting summary, 1999. http://sunsite.berkeley.edu/ Imaging/Databases/Metadata/niso-4-99-summary/

Besser, Howard and Anne Gilliland-Swetland. *Multimedia: Issues in Using Visual Material in Cultural Heritage Organizations*, Spring 1999 class and website. http://www.sims.berkeley.edu/impact/s99/

"Collecting at the Margins: Social Protest and Counterculture Materials,"
Collection Development Librarians of Academic Libraries Discussion, Jan.
30, 1999. American Library Association Midwinter 1999 Conference,
Philadelphia.

Commission on Preservation and Access (website).
http://www.clir.org/programs/cpa/cpa.html

Committee on Intellectual Property Rights and the Emerging Information
Infrastructure, National Research Council, National Academy of Sciences.
"The Digital Dilemma: Intellectual Property in the Information Age,"
Washington: National Academy Press, 2000.

CURL Exemplars in Digital Archives (website). http://www.leeds.ac.uk/cedars/

Internet Archive (website). http://www.archive.org

Lyman, Peter and Howard Besser. "Defining the Problem of our Vanishing
Memory: Background, Current Status, Models for Resolution" in Margaret
MacLean and Ben H. Davis, eds. *Time & Bits: Managing Digital Continuity,*
pp. 11-20, Los Angeles, CA: J. Paul Getty Trust, 1998.

MacLean, Margaret and Ben H. Davis, eds. *Time & Bits: Managing Digital
Continuity,* Los Angeles: J. Paul Getty Trust, 1998.

Making of America II White Paper (1998). http://sunsite.berkeley.edu/moa2/

Networked European Deposit Library (website). http://www.konbib.nl/nedlib/

Sanders, Terry. *Into the Future: Preservation of Information in the Electronic Age*
(16 mm film, 60 minutes). Santa Monica, CA: American Film Foundation,
1997.

Task Force on Archiving of Digital Information. *Preserving Digital Information,*
Commission on Preservation and Access and Research Libraries Group,
1996. http://www.rlg.org/ArchTF/tfadi.index.htm

X
Scholar Commentary: An End-User Speaks Up

Charles Rhyne
Reed College

I speak as a scholar-teacher. With my colleagues and students, I am dependent on the great storehouses of information in libraries, archives, and museums. Most of the time we take these resources for granted, but when a document we need is missing, we recognize how dependent we are on these materials and how grave is their loss or destruction. Occasionally, we reflect on the foresight of those who established these institutions and applaud the judgment of those who acquired, organized, and have cared for these materials. We also admire the complex, behind-the-scenes activity that makes these diverse materials available to so many users with such varied interests and needs.

Just now a student has begun a senior thesis with me on the famous pre-Columbian site at Monte Albán, which she discovered last year on a television program and hopes to visit in the near future. Waiting for her in the library are shelves of books filled with text and illustrations, articles in popular magazines and professional journals, catalogs of exhibitions, and newspaper articles on microfilm and microfiche. Several hundred original color slides taken on site are housed in the Art History Department, available for classroom use and student projects. Fifteen minutes away, related artifacts are on display in the Portland Art Museum.

Most Digital Materials Are Unreliable as Evidence

Now, of course, digital materials are also available for her to study, on CD-ROMs and the World Wide Web. But there is a striking difference between these new digital materials and the traditional analog materials on which we have relied in the past. To put it simply, only a few of these digital materials are reliable as evidence. The commercial hype surrounding computer use has produced CD-ROMs so shallow in content and so poor in image quality that very few would have been published in print. A search for any subject on the World Wide

Web produces a dizzying array of sites, most with inventive graphic design, amateurish text, and tourist photographs posted at low resolution. Happily, a rapidly increasing number of high quality sites are being posted on the Web, most based on original materials in the collections of museums, universities, and research institutes. But even here, the images are rarely available over the Internet at high resolution, and even these will be viewed on monitors of unpredictable sizes and viewing characteristics, generally adjusted for speed rather than quality. Only on the most advanced Web sites can the viewer know what s/he is looking at, and even this may be altered or disappear without notice. The unreliable material flooding most of the Web and the lack of recognized standards for judging it has delayed the acceptance of digital publication in evaluating the professional work of faculty at colleges and universities and has not encouraged serious scholars to get involved.

Few Scholar-Teachers Are Involved

For this we are all very much to blame. We are witnessing an immense transformation in the creation, retention, availability, and use of our cultural record, which is already transforming the way we understand our world. One might expect that all intellectually alive human beings at educational and research institutions would recognize the unique opportunity of participating in, possibly even contributing to, such a sweeping historical transformation. Few of us faculty have involved ourselves deeply, however, and, dare one say, too few of us have been asked.

Most of us now make use of email, perhaps we have developed Web pages for our classes and, especially where grant money has been available, we may have posted material from our research for student projects. But otherwise we sit on the sidelines, observing, following, sometimes complaining about the Internet as "a black hole" or the control of the digital world by engineers. We have not made

it clear that different disciplines have different needs, that there are certain basic needs that must be met if the digitized material is actually to be used, and that the standards and procedures being adopted by technology and information specialists may not provide for our students, fellow teachers, and research colleagues. This is a great loss, because the future of the digital world has a great deal to gain from the active involvement of end users at every stage of the process and a great deal to lose if we continue to follow at a distance.

Leading Prototypes

Some areas of the research community — most notably, space, military, and medical research — well funded by government and foundation programs, have been in the forefront of digital developments. Occasionally, the rest of the academic community and the public profit from their innovations, but the primary lesson to be learned is that digital projects in these fields have been directed to provide for the particular needs of their end-users. In these fields, end-users have been sought out and have been deeply involved at every stage of the process.

In the Humanities and Social Sciences, a few impressive prototypes also have been developed with foundation funding, propelled by recognition of the potential of the digital revolution. In the leading examples, national libraries and archives, major universities, and research institutes have begun digitizing their rare materials with high standards, recognizing that it is dangerous to handle rare documents often, expensive to redigitize, and impossible to predict the questions people may ask of these documents in the future. A notable feature of the best prototypes is that leading scholars and curators of the material have joined forces with computer specialists, often producing not only innovative ways to record and access the digital results but also new insights into the primary material, constituting advances in scholarship.

Photographic Images

As an art historian, I am especially aware of the uses we make of photographs of art and architecture, the most essential documentation in our field. Thus, I am especially aware of the characteristics we need in digital images of photographs if they are to be useful as study material for students and as research material for scholars. Let me use the rapidly expanding world of digital images to describe some of the current defects and the immense potential for the future.

> In the academy, words have always been privileged over images.

Frequently, when looking at images of works of art on computer monitors, I comment on the lack of detail, the inability to see the way an arch is constructed or to distinguish brush strokes in a painting. Often this is seen as a petty complaint, an unreasonable expectation for computer images. To address this I sometimes call up images of maps. Here, although my desire to see the shape of a hill or the location of a lake may be brushed aside, as soon as I point out that the words identifying these features are illegible, there is instant agreement that the digital image needs to be captured and made available at higher resolution.

In the academy, words have always been privileged over images. But in society at large, photography has claimed a larger and larger place on the front pages of newspapers and in magazines, not to mention on television, and the academy is gradually adjusting. Professional journals contain more and larger illustrations, increasingly in color, reflecting not only the reduced price of reproduction but also the major role now played by photography and film in many academic disciplines. Contemporary biology, medicine, and archaeology are heavily dependent on photographic imagery, and increasingly history, anthropology, and other social sciences have discovered the wealth of unstudied information waiting to be discovered in photographs. What is that person holding? What is the sign in that store window? What did people wear when attending that event? As a result, the acquisition and preservation of photographs is becoming as important as the preservation of words.

> We need visual searching tools comparable to those for text.

Likewise, computer search by keywords and category names, so useful for text, serves for searching photographs only when the photograph already has been labeled with the keyword the viewer wishes to locate. As photo archivists know so well, this is an immensely labor-intensive process requiring a degree of expertise in the subject matter; moreover, it is impossible to predict all the categories that will be of interest to future scholars. In addition to verbal searches, many end-users need visual search procedures. Not only artists teaching basic design or architects teaching urban housing, but also botanists searching for certain traits in leaf structure or anthropologists searching for varieties of body ornamentation need visual search tools. It would be more useful to be able to scan thousands of photographs of textiles around the world for certain weaving patterns than to expect every photo archivist to have entered the correct names for every pattern on every textile photograph. Difficult as it may be to achieve, we need visual searching tools comparable in range and specificity to those for text.

Traditional Standards of Evidence

The professional standards for evidence developed in every discipline through professional peer review and debate over the decades continue to hold. Whereas new, improved computer products appear constantly and are rapidly upgraded, research and teaching goals evolve slowly, based on successful approaches currently in use. It is not a natural fit. The challenge is to be open to the dramatic new possibilities of digital technology without being misled by unrestrained enthusiasm for the new technology. This requires above all that we have a firm grounding in our disciplines and a long-term view of what we hope to accomplish in our research, teaching, and the broader dissemination of information and ideas.

Students and scholars will use some digital material because it is readily available on their institution's computers but not in their libraries. The ability of computers to make text and images available worldwide is one of the essential break-throughs of the computer revolution. In the long run, however, for serious scholarship (including term papers, master's, and doctoral theses being written at thousands of colleges and universities every year), digital material will substitute for print material only when it meets the same standards of accuracy and reliability. At present this is far from the case. However, new professional journals are beginning to be published online, peer-reviewed with the same standards as traditional printed journals; and students are gradually being trained to discriminate among online publications in the same way that they have learned to discriminate among print material. Librarians are essential players in this educational process.

Supposed Defects Can Be Turned into Assets

However, we should not settle for matching previous standards because these were themselves often defective. For example, we often hear the complaint that digital images of photographs can easily be changed without the viewer being aware — but this was true also of photographs themselves (notwithstanding that many changes to photographs were clumsy and therefore easily detected). Digital technology actually offers us the possibility of recording these changes automatically for the first time. This is, in fact, what is needed if digital images of photographs are to serve as evidence. We need a system that provides for the automatic recording of the creation of and changes to each image within the digital record of the image.

Perhaps this may encourage us to record also what we should have been doing all along, the way in which each photograph is made. We now have cameras that record on the film or digital record the date and time each photograph was made, at least if the date and time are set correctly. But we need to know also the type of camera, lens, and film used. It is now a commonplace that no photograph is the single accurate image of a subject. Everything depends on the lighting, the angle of view, distance from the subject, and of course the characteristics of the film and lens. Many of these things are reasonably visible in the photograph itself, but many are not. To the extent that these can now be recorded automatically in the data that is part of the digital record for each image, there is the opportunity of making images of photographs more reliable as evidence than has been the case in the past.

> Digital images can be made more reliable as evidence . . .

Digital imagery could make possible other significant advances. To give one example, careful reading of scholarly articles in professional journals in all disciplines that depend upon photographs as evidence is flawed by the inadequacy of the illustrations. The reproductions are too few in number, too small, and too seldom done with accurate color. It has been too expensive to publish the large body of photographs on which the text depends. In many cases, readers must take the arguments on faith or suspend judgment. The illustrations simply do not allow one to test the assertions made about them. But it is much less expensive to publish large, high quality color images on the Web. It would now be possible to publish articles fully illustrated on the Web with high quality reproductions of all the photographs on which the research depended. Likewise, we can now include appendices of the detailed data on which much research depends.

A Fully Participatory Society

I have no doubt that the digital revolution is one of the great information revolutions in the history of humankind, fully comparable to the invention of printing and the invention of photography, but taking place at dramatic speed. We are privileged to be alive with the opportunity to witness this transformation, to experience it, and even to participate in its development. Indeed, only if all elements of society do participate in its development will it fulfill its immense potential. In deciding what materials to digitize, how to preserve them, and how to make them available, let us recognize the serious interest of the public in all area of human knowledge, the public's right to know, and the great untapped resource that these materials provide. The digital revolution offers us our first opportunity for a fully participatory society.

Index: Handbook for Digital Projects

fair use, 72–74
laws governing, 66–69
notice requirements, 69–70
Web sites for information about, 79–82
works for hire, 70–71
See also U.S. Copyright Act
correction handling procedures, and vendors, 152–153
costs. *See* economic issues
custody and digital longevity issues, 160–161
See also provenance

D

defamation issues, 75
derivative works and copyright, 69
deselection, Nomination Form for Deselection, 53–54
despeckling images, 95–96
digital asset management, 117
digital cameras, CCDs and CMOS chips in, 84
digital imaging technology
advantages of digital access, 6
digitization process, 83
image measures, 85–93
image processing, 94–100
preservation purposes of, 9–11
reformatting comparison, 100–101
risks of, 7
technical primer on, 83–102
transformative nature of, 7–8
Digital Millennium Copyright Act (DMCA), 67
digital mortgage, 37
digital preservation, defined, 7
digital-to-digital conversions, translation problems, 161–162
digital values for pixels, measuring, 93
dithering, 97
DMCA (Digital Millennium Copyright Act), 67
documents for project planning, 26
donors
donor-restricted material, 38
See also stakeholders
dots per inch (DPI), 86
DPI (dots per inch), 86
drum scanners, PMTs in, 84
duration of copyright, 70, 71

E

economic issues
budget phase of project planning, 28–29
capital investment, 7
cost estimates, 32
metadata creation costs, 38
microfilm digitization costs, 130–131
OCR costs, 112
on-going costs (the digital mortgage), 37
photograph digitization, 117–118
research community funding and digital proto-types, 168–169
scanning and keying of text, 104–105
scanning technology capabilities, 11–12
text digitization quality and cost decisions, 108–110
Electronic Communications Decency Act, 75
emulation software for viewing old file formats, 160, 163–164
encoded text, 105
encryption schemes, long-term effects of, 158–159
end users. *See* users
evaluation of nominated materials, 36
Checklist for Evaluation, 55–59
the process, 41
sample evaluation, 42–43
evidence
standards for, 170–171
unreliability of digital materials as, 167–168
evidential value, 44

F

fair use, 72–74
federal agencies
employees and public domain works, 70
Freedom of Information Act and, 76
file sizes
compression types, 100
long-term effects of compression, 158
for oversized documents, 124
preservation quality scans of photographs, 88
file structure, 99–100
filters, 94
finding aids
linking and preservation for intellectual integrity, 15
searching tools needed for images, 170
fixation and copyright, 66, 69

R

S

T

text. *See* printed text
thresholding, 95–96
tonal controls, 97
tonal scale comparisons, 98–99
tone reproduction, photographs, 115
transcending original sources, 10
transformative use, fair use and, 72, 73
translation problem, digital-to-digital conversions, 161–162
true (optical) resolution, 87

U

unreliability of digital materials as evidence, 167–168
unsharp mask filter, 94
URL file location changes, long-term access problems, 159–160
U.S. Constitution, and copyright, 66
U.S. Copyright Act
    basic protections of, 69
    Digital Millennium Copyright Act (DMCA), 67
    early amendments to, 66
    fair use, 72
    Sonny Bono Term Extension Act, 70
    Visual Artists Rights Act (VARA), 68
use, and prioritization of materials, 46–47
users
    academic end-user commentary, 167–172
    access problems for scanned large maps, 125
    and development of functional requirements, 24

V

value, and prioritization of materials, 44–45
value judgments and preservation selection, 13–14
VARA (Visual Artists Rights Act), 68
vector images, 84
vendors
    assessing bids from, 148–150
    benefits of using, 143–144
    choosing, 144–148
    correction handling procedures, 152–153
    microfilm digitization services, 131–132
    microfilm scanning systems, 132–133
    quality control issues, 152–153
    working and communicating with, 151–152
Visual Artists Rights Act (VARA), 68

W

wavelet compression, 100
Web-safe color palette, 93
Web sites
    legal information references, 79–82
    long-term access problems due to file location changes, 159–160
    for map scanning, 126
    microfilm conversion services, 131–132
    microfilm scanning system vendors, 132–133
WIPO (World Intellectual Property Organization), 67
workflow management, 29–31
works for hire, 70–71
World Intellectual Property Organization (WIPO), 67